CW00551087

RUDOLF STEINER (1861–1925) called his spiritual philosophy 'anthroposophy', meaning 'wisdom of the human being'. As a highly developed seer, he based his work on direct knowledge and perception of spiritual dimensions. He initiated a modern and universal 'science of spirit', accessible to anyone willing to exercise clear and unprejudiced thinking.

From his spiritual investigations Steiner provided suggestions for the renewal of many activities, including education (both general and special), agriculture, medicine, economics, architecture, science, philosophy, religion and the arts. Today there are thousands of schools, clinics, farms and other organizations involved in practical work based on his principles. His many published works feature his research into the spiritual nature of the human being, the evolution of the world and humanity, and methods of personal development. Steiner wrote some 30 books and delivered over 6000 lectures across Europe. In 1924 he founded the General Anthroposophical Society, which today has branches throughout the world.

GROWING OLD

The Spiritual Dimensions of Ageing

RUDOLF STEINER

Selected texts with commentaries by Franz Ackermann

RUDOLF STEINER PRESS

Translated by Matthew Barton

Rudolf Steiner Press,
Hillside House, The Square
Forest Row, RH18 5ES

www.rudolfsteinerpress.com

Published by Rudolf Steiner Press 2019

© Futurum Verlag 2018
This translation © Rudolf Steiner Press 2019

All rights reserved. Apart from any fair dealing for the purpose of private
study, research, criticism or review, as permitted under the Copyright,
Designs and Patents Act, 1988, no part of this publication may be
reproduced, stored in a retrieval system, or transmitted in any form or by
any means, electronic, electrical, chemical, mechanical, optical,
photocopying, recording or otherwise, without the prior written
permission of the copyright owner. Inquiries should be addressed to the
Publishers

A catalogue record for this book is available from the British Library

Print book ISBN: 978 1 85584 562 6
Ebook ISBN: 978 1 85584 505 3

Cover by Morgan Creative
Typeset by DP Photosetting, Neath, West Glamorgan
Printed and bound by 4Edge Ltd., Essex

Contents

Introduction

We all grow old. And this begs questions: What happens as we age? When are we old? What can we expect of old age? How will we cope with it? The present volume seeks to address these questions. It is intended for all who see our human existence as an adventure, right up to the last moment, and old age itself as harbouring treasures we can discover as long as we don't dismiss it as the mere failing of capacities. Concerns about our 'ageing population' can then be set against a true sense of the fruits of old age. If we grow old consciously, and learn to make something of our ageing, seeing it not only as physical decline but as a period when we still participate in—and indeed, still help shape—life, then we can find existential meaning in it.

Ageing takes courage. And trust. Can we think of our life in its complexity and development other than in ways defined by the narrow corset of our modern scientific and medical paradigms? In his carefully developed science of the soul and spirit, Rudolf Steiner offered us stimulus for broadening and enlarging these habits of thought which seem to hold us in their thrall. His path of schooling can help us toward a different outlook. And the idea of recurring lives on earth allows us to develop a different attitude toward old age and death. The book starts here, and opens up other perspectives on our ageing, with a far-reaching view of the transformative processes in which human beings and the earth itself are involved.

To compile this volume, I sifted through a wealth of written and verbal comments in the works of Rudolf Steiner.

Some readers may react with scepticism to the spiritual depths of what is presented. But if you can keep an open mind, allowing yourself to enter into the broad scope of earthly and cosmic development as here conveyed, insights into the meaning and importance of old age can dawn, and open up new dimensions.

The book approaches the many-layered issue of ageing from different angles. Wide-ranging cosmological perspectives alternate with detailed and differentiated observations of the specific phenomena of ageing, and their connection with the rest of our life. The anthroposophic outlook characteristically regards ageing as part of a larger context, connected with an evolutionary process encompassing all forms of existence, both earthly and cosmic. Chapter 1 examines this. The following chapter then goes on to deal with characteristic phenomena of human ageing as Steiner regards them. Following these basic aspects of an anthroposophic gerontology, Chapter 3 offers a more extensive survey of overall development, firstly in relation to historical and cultural evolution and then in terms of individual human biography. The various stages of life, and the changes we either succeed or fail in achieving, are important milestones toward a wholesome ageing process. Independence at the end of life is a principle much vaunted in modern gerontology. Freedom is the highest human possession, and involves both opportunities and dangers, and hence we can speak positively of an 'art of ageing'. As far as the dangers are concerned, Chapter 4 details not only typical infirmities but also some potentially pathological phenomena of old age. Steiner's account of dementia offers a surprising angle on this widespread concern. Transformations in the fabric of body, soul and spirit are, ultimately, very diverse, and culminate in the process of dying as a release from bodily conditions. In the chapter on 'Ageing and Death' we find a description of the human corpse as offered by anthroposophy's broader view, and also an account of what happens after we cross the threshold of death.

The fruitful relationship between childhood and old age is a theme running through the book. Dialogue between the generations and the potential of these relationships is receiving more attention nowadays. How space can be made for such interactions in daily life and how, in particular, family and school life can have a decisive effect on our health and vitality in old age, is considered in the chapter on ageing as an educational challenge. The book begins with the primary meaning that ageing has in evolutionary terms, and it ends with a consideration of the human being as co-creator in cosmic processes, and with our capacity to become increasingly conscious of the tasks this implies.

Many years as a director of state-funded care and nursing homes for the elderly have given the compiler of this volume first-hand knowledge both of current practices and of research in conventional and anthroposophic gerontology. His experiences with the elderly and the dying, involving many rich and diverse human encounters but also knowledge of prevailing concepts, have fed into this volume and govern the selection and compilation of texts. The suggestions and insights which Rudolf Steiner offered on this theme around a century ago, based on his spiritual-scientific investigations, are thus geared to questions that still preoccupy us today. The last chapter contains pointers toward further, hopefully fruitful dialogue.

Finally, I'd like to make a general remark about this kind of thematic anthology: the passages collected here are drawn from many different contexts, usually either from public lectures or ones given in more intimate circles, and are always excerpts from a 'whole' that was addressed to a very specific audience at the time. They have been placed into a new context in this volume, to highlight the diversity and relevance of ideas this book seeks to illumine. That each excerpt originally belonged in its particular setting should always be remembered, and this volume is therefore also conceived as a stimulus for further reading.

The Core Messages of Ageing

It seems fitting to start with essential and general principles before going on to speak of specific details of ageing. An overall holistic view of the ageing process will enable us to discern and understand its significance. At the same time this highlights an important principle in this book: that a deeper meaning, a message, is intrinsic to ageing. Forearmed with this insight, it will be easier for us to accept ageing in each individual instance, as part of an all-embracing process. Ageing as such manifests throughout the cosmos, and human ageing is only a special instance of this.

All existence is subject to ageing processes. Nothing arises without going under again, and as it does so something new emerges. Ageing therefore also signifies transformation, evolution. And evolution means that something higher develops through this transformation. From this perspective, death is an expression of something overcome on whose foundation a higher life germinates.

The cosmos also ages and evolves. Here too, evolution means transformation into a higher condition. This holds true for planetary embodiments and for the hierarchies of angels. In the divine world of spirit, beings aspire toward ever richer forms of consciousness. Rudolf Steiner perceived these dimensions and described them in various ways. Of particular note here is the detailed way in which, drawing on Dionysius the Areopagite's Christian doctrine of angelic hierarchies, Steiner described the characteristics of the hosts of spirit beings—from angeloi and archangeloi through to cherubim and seraphim—highlighting their specific tasks for Creation and for the further evolution of cosmos and human being.[1]

Life is accompanied by *maturation processes* which end and are acknowledged in diverse ways: school readiness, puberty and coming of age are the best-known thresholds in human life through which we pass to become adults. Unfortunately, we often overlook other but no less important developmental stages. Those privileged to encounter the elderly at first hand know however that processes of maturation accompany life up to our very last breath.

Extinction is already implicit in blossoming. Yet this development is by no means either linear or final in nature. Subtler observation shows, rather, that fertilization occurs; that in blossoming something emerges that will not go to the grave but will ripen again toward a higher existence.

For this kind of transformation to occur, we need human community. We only become fully human through other people, as we know from the field of education. That this principle of reciprocity must not fade in the evening of life comes to expression wherever people are trying to create a new 'culture of care'. 'Beyond ensuring we ourselves receive care, such a culture is founded on caring about and for others', said the well-known Heidelberg gerontologist Andreas Kruse,[2] chair of the Berlin commission on ageing which published its extensive report in the 1990s.

On 5 December 1912, Rudolf Steiner gave a lecture, at the Architect's House in Berlin, entitled 'Life Questions and the Enigma of Death Illumined through Spiritual Research'. Concluding the lecture, he summed up his comments in a kind of mantra or verse which, it seems to me, can well serve as a guiding thought and introduction to this anthology.

Everything alive in the cosmos
lives only by creating within itself
the germ of new life.
And the soul gives itself up to ageing and to death
only in order to ripen immortally
to ever new life.[3]

Ageing as the foundation of all evolution

In his fundamental work *Occult Science, an Outline*, published in 1909, Rudolf Steiner devoted a whole chapter to the evolution of the human being and the world. In doing so he formulated the following underlying law of development:

> All evolution is in fact founded on this: that independent being first separates itself out from the life of its surroundings, these surroundings then imprinting themselves on this separate being like a reflection, after which this separate being evolves further independently.[4]

This law can likewise be applied to human life and ageing: at birth we are separated from a cosmic totality, and the ageing process begins with our development as independent beings on the earth. In the process, through thinking, we gradually inform or imprint our thinking with something resembling substance: the cosmic wisdom we make our own. It is precisely in this that the maturation process consists. At death, what we acquired during life on earth is carried back into the cosmos, and made available to it for its own independent further evolution.

It does not come easily to us to imagine that our existence has been of a quite different nature in every era, and will be different again in future. But this is what distinguishes us from animals: we are continually developing, and learning new things from one life to the next.

Nowadays people have no sense at all that they are living beings who evolve through time. Instead they feel they are something timeless. People speak today of 'the human being' without paying heed to our developing nature, to the fact that we draw something new into our whole evolution at every stage of life.[5]

Only when we adopt this outlook can we gain a new relationship to time and thus to human evolution and development. To do so we have to include the idea that humankind originates in the macrocosm. The eternal core of our being enters the body which becomes available to it as 'outward form'. Rudolf Steiner speaks of this in his lecture of 11 December 1920. Only around the middle of our life do we gradually start to transform physical corporeality into spirit and soul. This is accompanied at the same time by degenerative processes that will ultimately lead to death. We increasingly become estranged from our body, as part of the natural course of development. And yet human freedom implies the possibility of a turnaround, of initiating a maturation process. Steiner's exacting observations below culminate in the insight that human existence only comes into its own in the presence of freedom and love.

People think that the human embryo grows simply within the mother's body, nourished by the forces of her body itself, only because their outward sight cannot perceive how the whole macrocosm is involved in this; only because they do not see the influences playing in from without so that the human being is here truly connected with the whole macrocosm. In fact this human embryo clearly comes from the world of spirit, merely making use of this habitation in which it finds the gateway, if you like, for entering the physical world. In all that surrounds us in spatial conditions no gateway can be found—except within the human body itself—for the human being who has passed through the period between death and a new birth to enter the physical world. And the forces active there are not those of father and mother, but cosmic forces seeking their approach to the physical world through the mother's body after fertilization, once the being of spirit and soul has developed the desire for this.

Thus the human being is transformed into a physical being, but this physical being is only the outward form for something spiritual in nature. We see that the child initially possesses, let us say, undifferentiated features, and that the human form increasingly develops from this. But we would be wrong to say that there is something emerging and developing from within the child as such. Rather, we should turn our gaze from the child back to what was active before birth, before conception, and continues to work on: to what expresses its activity in the child. Our observations of the child from day to day, from week to week and from year to year will show us the influx of a past condition through which the human soul and spirit passed before birth or conception. We only observe the child rightly if we see their particular qualities developing not from within the child's organization itself but in antecedents whose light still shines into the child. The failure to do so is the great misfortune of our modern outlook. The important thing is to draw help from the past, conceiving it as still active in our present. And as we follow the further development of life through time, we can keep returning from physical corporeality, transforming it back, into spirit and soul. As we became physical human beings, the spirit and soul did actually transform itself into physical corporeality, and now we transform this physical corporeality back into spirit and soul again. You will point out a difficulty here. We could understand how physical corporeality transforms back into spirit and soul if this occurred gradually, so that, let us say, we saw that a person had become entirely physical around the age of 35 and then began to grow spiritual again, and by the end of their life had been spiritualized to such a degree that death would be merely a slow transition back into spirit and soul. This does indeed happen inwardly, but not outwardly, and here we are deceived by appearances. In our declining years—and the somewhat older people in the audience will I hope not take this amiss—we bear our body with us as something of a burden, as something that no longer entirely belongs to us. We slowly become a corpse, and death consists only in the fact that this corpse of ours grows too heavy, that gravity becomes too strong when, on awakening each morning, our soul comes back into this body. But if we direct our senses only to outward appearance, we cannot discern these changes already occurring in us, do not notice that this second half of life is already a gradual dying.

Rather than merely assuming the existence of spirit and soul on the one hand, and physical corporeality on the other, we should learn to see how, when we gain help from the concept of time, spirit and soul transform into physical corporeality, and physical corporeality in turn transforms itself back into spirit and soul. Although this gives only outward expression to the course of human evolution, it is connected with two significant human attributes. What enables us to metamorphose slowly from a spirit-soul condition into a physical and corporeal one so that we become physical and bodily in nature, so that we become one with physical corporeality? We can grasp this when we come to understand the moral quality of love. The following is an important and fundamental truth: we enter the physical world through love, by pouring ourselves into physical corporeality. And how do we depart again? We withdraw ourselves again from this physical, corporeal metamorphosis, we transform ourselves back, and the power that enables us to undertake this re-transformation is none other than freedom. In other words, our further development, made possible by passing through death, occurs precisely through freedom. We are born through cosmic love, and we pass through the gateway of death into the world of spirit and soul through the power of freedom that we have within us. If we develop love in the world, this love is basically the echo, the continuing resonance of our being of spirit and soul as we possessed it before birth, or let us say before conception. And if we develop freedom in our existence between birth and death, soul-spiritually we are prefiguring development of the power that will be most important to us once we have departed from the body at death.

In cosmic terms, what does it actually mean to be a free being? To be a free being, to be able to transform ourselves back from physical corporeality into spirit and soul, actually means to be able to die. Love, on the other hand, means being able to transform ourselves from the realm of spirit and soul into that of physical corporeality. In cosmic terms, being able to love means being able to live.

As you see, occurrences that doubtless also can be seen in entirely naturalistic terms, being born and departing from the body, birth and death, which external scientists see only as natural processes, can be understood as manifestations of love and freedom. And by developing love out of our will in a soul-spiritual sense, what are we actually doing? We are creating a soul-spiritual after-image within us, within our skin, of what constituted our whole being before we were conceived. Before our conception we live in the cosmos through the power of love. And the development of love as a moral virtue during life between birth and death is in a sense a memory of this cosmic life in our feeling and will. The virtue of love appears like a refinement within the microcosm of what is spread out macrocosmically before birth; and awareness of our freedom arises in us because, during our life between birth and death, we bear within us soul-spiritually something that will act fully in the cosmos, like the workings of a natural power, after we have passed through the portal of death. We experience love and freedom between birth and death. They are nothing other than the human echoes of cosmic powers, cosmic love being associated with all birth, and cosmic freedom with all death. Since the natural sciences became predominant, we have been speaking of all kinds of natural forces—light, heat, electricity and so on. But we do not speak of the natural forces—or it would be better to say the cosmic forces—that lead us into physical, sense existence as human beings, and out of it again. Consider for a moment the fields of physics, chemistry and biology, and think of all the forces constituting the world described in these terms. Such forces can explain everything in the world that is not human, but they can never explain the nature of human beings on earth. You see, for the human being to exist here, freedom and love are needed as well as the actions of electricity, light, heat and so on in the world. If we engage in this way of thinking, and really learn to understand human nature, we can form concepts of natural creatures which are simultaneously moral and natural concepts. And then we no longer have two distinct and unconnected realms: of morality, on the one hand, and the natural world on the other, with no bridge between them.[6]

In his lecture of 25 August 1911, Steiner now describes the beginnings of cosmic-earthly evolution from a quite different perspective. He begins with the evolution of Saturn in the long-distant past, a remote, primordial time in which physical conditions were as yet present only in the form of warmth or energy. In Greek myths, this primordial wisdom reappears in a vivid, pictorial language.

As Saturn evolution was beginning, or, more accurately, before it began, the ether stream of all humanity and all earthly evolution of which we spoke was as yet a single one. At the moment when Saturn evolution starts, dichotomy, duality arises within the powers of the macrocosm. We will consider later why this happened, but for now we will simply identify it as a fact. Duality is initiated in all macrocosmic activity only at the moment when Saturn evolution begins. Greek mythology interprets duality in terms of the opposition or enmity between ancient Saturn, or Chronos as the Greeks called him, and his father, Uranus. This legend shows an awareness of the original unity of all macrocosmic powers. But as old Saturn or Chronos began to crystallize, something that intimately pertains to this Chronos opposed universal evolution. Duality arose; and if we stay for now with what simply occurred, we can say that the totality of divine-spiritual beings who held sway when Saturn evolution commenced, divided inwardly in a sense, giving us an evolutionary stream directly involved in everything that has unfolded from Saturn through Sun and Moon evolution to our present Earth stage, on the one hand, and another stream alongside this primary one.[7]

> Human ageing will now be considered from a further, and again different, perspective, that of the ageing of the earth and cosmos. This cosmological dimension of ageing will be taken up again at the end of the book and examined in detail.

Our earth, with everything upon it, has already entered upon its period of decline, its decadence. I have often mentioned that even knowledgeable geologists recognize this fact. We can demonstrate purely outwardly, physically, with very rigorous and precise geology, that the earth is already breaking down, that the rising trajectory of its evolution has ended and we are in fact walking around on a rupturing earth-slab. And it is not just the mineral earth that is breaking down, but all organic life too is declining—the structures of plants, the bodies of animals and humans are no longer in rising evolution but are degenerating.[8]

The meaning of ageing

As we mature, our human existence acquires meaning and fulfilment. Evolution toward ever higher stages of consciousness is associated with this. On earth we develop self-awareness that kindles in resistance to the sense world, as we can observe when we wake up each day: our I experiences bodily reality as an external world, and it awakens to its surroundings through the sense organs. Rudolf Steiner distinguishes three levels or 'sheaths' into which the I enters on its path toward birth, each being of a different 'substance'. We develop alert awareness through the soul nature of the astral body, we acquire life through the etheric body, and receive physical form through the mineral body that decays as corpse at death. Our I consciousness grows through the resistance of these corporeal sheaths, and this wears them out, eventually leading to death. And yet our truly human nature develops through these ageing and death processes. Rudolf Steiner spoke on this theme in 1912/13 in numerous European cities. The lectures are compiled in a volume entitled *Esoteric Investigations into the Life Between Death and Rebirth.*

From the time when I consciousness is present, the I pushes against our own inner corporeality, and begins to live inwards. It begins to come up against our own body within. If you want to picture this, you need only think of the child waking up each morning. Here the I and the astral body enter the physical and etheric body, the I nudging into the physical and etheric body. If you imagine the resistance you feel when you put your hand in water and push it through, something similar happens when the I submerges itself in the morning and finds itself bathed in its interior life. Throughout life, this I is sunk in the physical and etheric body, and pushes against these bodies on all sides. If you splash your hand about in water, you become aware of its every part; and the same is true when the I immerses itself in the etheric body and physical body, nudging into every part of this corporeality. This happens throughout life. During the whole of life we have to submerge ourselves each morning in our physical body and etheric body, and by doing so the physical body and etheric body on the one hand, and the astral body and I on the other, continually impinge on, or collide with each other. And the consequence of this? The colliding entities wear away, are worn down. What happens under continual impact between two material bodies also happens between the I and the astral body, on the one hand, and the etheric and physical body on the other. They wear each other out—and this is why we gradually age; this is why we increasingly wear out throughout life, and this is also why we physically die. If we had no physical or etheric body, we would not be able to sustain our I consciousness either. We would still be able to *develop* I consciousness, but could not *sustain* it. You see, we always have to push ourselves inward, come up against resistance within if the I is to be sustained in our awareness. From this—an extraordinarily significant fact—it follows that the development of our I arises from the destruction of our being. If the aspects or levels of our being did not come up against each other, did not collide as they do, we could not have I consciousness. And if people ask why they age and perish, then we have to reply that we develop as we wear ourselves out, or more precisely, I consciousness keeps developing, and that is the reason for ageing and dying. To put this in the most radical terms, if we could not die, we could not be truly human either. And if we allow the full importance of this fact to work upon our soul, the following thought can emerge, one which finds an answer in esotericism: to live as human beings we always need the physical body, etheric body, astral body and I. As we are constituted today, we need these four 'members'. And yet in order to acquire I consciousness, we have to destroy them. We have to keep acquiring them in order to destroy them again. This is why recurring lives on earth are necessary—so that we become able to keep repeatedly destroying our human bodies, and thereby keep evolving further as conscious human beings.[9]

> According to Steiner, the process of growth and decay conceals the 'secret of all life'. In a process of continual self-vanquishing the human soul grows victorious over physical form.

There is something in nature that continually destroys and overcomes one form of life through another. Those who can sense this will also—to choose this most exemplary of instances—be able to feel that the configurations of the natural human form contain something mysterious: that in each moment this form, which realizes itself in outer life, is in fact killed by a higher life. That is the secret of all life: continually and everywhere a lower life is killed by a higher one. This human form of ours, permeated by the human soul, by human life, is continually killed, continually overcome, by the human soul, by human life. And this occurs in a way that can be stated like this: the human form as such bears something that would be entirely different if it were left to its own nature, if it could follow its own intrinsic life. But it cannot do so because it also possesses a higher, different life that continually kills this other intrinsic life.[10]

> Old age is not held in high regard nowadays, nor are the very particular experiences involved in it, which might actually inspire us. And yet the process of maturation could acquire huge importance in social co-existence, especially if we focused on the spiritual development connected with it. In his lecture on 21 May 1918, Rudolf Steiner makes a plea for us to value growing old, pointing to the impulses that could arise from intergenerational encounters.

Who nowadays believes in the productivity, the fruitfulness of growing older? And since people don't, it has none. They are not attentive to how each new year brings new revelations. But consider how much would change in human life if this belief gained general currency—if everyone recognized they must wait to be older, and would then learn things at first hand that they could not know before. Where do we find expectancy and hope today? Yet if such a thought and feeling entered the life of society, think what a huge significance it would have. What huge significance it would have if, alongside what I will call the 'egalitarian demolitions' at work nowadays in all sorts of areas, an awareness grew in community life that simply by virtue of growing to be 40 we can learn things that we cannot know when we're 27. If this sense of things became natural and customary, imagine what it could mean for the way a 27-year-old relates to a 40-year-old. Of course there is no chance of this happening at present, since 60-year-olds are often no older than 27. Even those in the highest positions are no older, but fail to notice the fact. Today therefore, we can't urge such a thing as a reality.

And yet that is what life must bring and what the future requires: that people begin to regard the spirit as a reality again. The only way in which, in general, people acknowledge the spirit today is as a sum of abstract concepts. A person nowadays develops a sum of abstract ideas, of the kind one can indeed easily assimilate by the age of 27.[11]

Fundamental Principles of Gerontology

Ageing is characterized by natural decline. That at least is how it seems at first glance. But if we take a closer look, we can also discern a regenerative current flowing in the middle of life: in fact the etheric body, or body of formative forces, grows ever younger, a dynamic of which Rudolf Steiner gave a precise account. Whereas the physical body ages over time, and becomes frail, during the course of life the etheric body grows ever more vigorous.

This 'growing younger' of the body of formative forces as Steiner describes it,[12] is of key importance for a full understanding of the processes connected with ageing. Although this idea appears unusual to begin with, the associated outlook on ageing it invokes is a strength of anthroposophic gerontology, which not only considers the physical decline of old age, but also the renewal that comes with it, the inner gains and riches acquired.

Something similar is true too of the 'growing younger' of humanity, a no less apt observation of Rudolf Steiner's. Over the millennia, the age at which the physical body concludes its development has shifted ever earlier into youth. The term 'acceleration' used for this, figures, in Steiner's terms, as the growing younger of humanity. Today, natural physical development, but also that of spirit and soul, ceases according to Steiner around the age of 27. Going back through history we find that this point at which the ageing process begins fell ever later in human life. Humanity remained younger for longer, as it were, or in other words the body retained its developmental capacity for longer. To balance the shifting of this threshold to an ever younger moment of life, we need to take intentional hold of the maturation process. Steiner describes corresponding ideal or typical developmental phases, and stresses that around the age of 35 we approach a moment in life—which we can also miss—that is decisive for successful ageing.

Of particular importance for the process and understanding of ageing, both individually and culturally, is the relationship between the generations. On many occasions Rudolf Steiner spoke of the interdependency of younger and older generations. To become open to developmental processes, both young and old need stimulus from those in the opposite phase of life. The echo of starry breadths that resonates into life through the gateway of birth acts like a reminder or admonition to old people. And the gateway of death, as a place where we embark on new existence, can demonstrate the riches of a fully lived life, and encourage younger people to ask questions about life and meaning. At the end of this chapter, Steiner examines the impulses that young and old offer each other. And in the chapter on 'Growing Old—a Challenge for Education', he looks once again at this theme from a different perspective.

What the different life phases signify for old age

In studying the different phases of life, we are first concerned primarily with physical development, and thus with the fundamental change from upbuilding development to decline. The human body of formative forces or etheric body is directly involved in this. But human spiritual reality passes through an opposite developmental process, as Rudolf Steiner described in a lecture on 21 May 1918.

But there is tangible spiritual reality involved in the fact that, in our life here on earth between birth and death, we first have flourishing, burgeoning life in the period of development that stops when we are 27, and then, from the age of 35, our forces begin to decline. This tangible spiritual reality changes just as we do outwardly, but has a more or less opposite trajectory to that of our external body. Outwardly we grow old, wrinkly; but our etheric body, our body of formative forces grows ever younger. Yet people today do not concern themselves with this body of formative forces that grows younger as we age. People get grey hair, go bald, and do not realize that their body of formative forces is gaining flourishing, burgeoning life just at the moment when they start getting grey hairs; that this is precisely when it can endow them with things which they could not acquire previously. Their ignorance of this is due to the nature of our era. But things need to change in this respect. Our times need a change of ideas. A change that is needed especially is that thoughts should grow a little more sound and vigorous, not clinging to mere outward appearances, for otherwise we will become terribly narrow and limited in all fields. It is vital to use thinking in such a way as to penetrate reality in a particular field.[13]

> Steiner describes the etheric body growing younger in a telling turn of phrase, saying that, by contrast, to physical shrinkage, it grows 'chubby-cheeked'.

We grow older, but in fact only our physical body grows older. From a spiritual perspective it is not true to say that we grow older. This is *maya*, outward illusion [...] This is true even in respect of the etheric body, which is invisible and supersensible, and which we carry with us between birth and death just as we carry our physical body of flesh, blood and bones. We bear this etheric body, or body of formative forces with us in the same way, but there is a difference between them. The physical body ages, while the etheric body or body of formative forces is old when we are born. If we enquire into its true nature, it is actually old at that moment, and grows ever younger. Thus we can say that this first spiritual aspect in us becomes ever more vigorous, ever younger, by contrast with our physical corporeality which grows weak and infirm. And it is actually literally true to say that as we start getting lines and wrinkles on our face, our etheric body begins to flourish, becomes chubby-cheeked.[14]

Through the forces that form it, our etheric body, if that is the term we wish to use, is old when conducted toward birth or conception. As we begin our physical life it is old—is highly formed and incised, with a great many inner configurations—these are motions but also inner configurations. During the course of life it loses these, but its vigour is enhanced, and when we die in old age, it is a child. Our etheric body therefore passes through precisely the opposite development from our physical body. If we say that the physical body ages, we have to say that the etheric body 'juvenates'. It is good to coin a term for this process at work in the etheric body. We really do 'juvenate' in relation to our etheric body. At the time we are born we have directed the strength of this body to all that is enclosed within our skin whereas, when we pass through the gateway of death at a certain age, it has a kind of affinity with the whole cosmos. It has regained the forces that it was deprived of. In our childhood, its connection with the cosmos was interrupted when it had to direct all its forces into the space enclosed solely by the human skin, being compressed into a single point in the world, as it were. Now it grows fresh and vigorous again, and is increasingly restored to the cosmos as the physical body ages. We can say—though this is of course greatly exaggerated—that as we grow bald and wrinkly, the etheric body becomes chubby-cheeked, and once again an image of outward power, of outwardly creative vigour, flourishing energy, just as the physical body is an expression of outward, flourishing, creative energy in early infancy. As far as our etheric body is concerned, we 'juvenate' during life.[15]

> We can observe development in the ageing process through history. In past times, the phase of maturity started in a different way and at a different period of life. In relation to these evolving changes, Rudolf Steiner spoke of 'humanity growing younger'. In his lecture of 21 May 1918, he described the evolutionary law corresponding to this: in ancient times people remained capable of development for longer. Nowadays this development lasts only until the age of 27, and then 'nothing more can be drawn from our physical aspect'. By contrast, soul-spiritual development becomes ever more important.

As we know, up to a certain age we develop quite naturally, without any effort on our part, through our innate physical forces. In the early period following the great Atlantean catastrophe, as we have said, human beings were capable of development for much longer—their natural development continued into their fifties. And they knew that as they grew older this was also connected with a transformation of their soul and spirit. But nowadays if we want to embark on development of soul and spirit after our twenties, we have to seek to do so by willpower, by effort. Until our twenties we change and develop physically, and in these changes at the same time lives something that determines our further soul-spiritual progress. The physical ceases to let us be dependent on it. And then nothing more can be drawn from our physical aspect, and instead we have to advance further by our own willpower. That is how it appears outwardly at least. In a moment we will take a look at how things are inwardly.[16]

Based on the evolutionary tendencies in humanity that I have often described, we believe nowadays that we have more or less reached the height of our powers by the age of 20 or so. We believe in our twenties that we are mature enough to be elected to serve on a city council or as a member of parliament, that we are able to deliberate and decide on everything. People today think that the old custom of waiting for a later age, for the greater experience and understanding each year brings, is a thing of the past. Nowadays we expect the child's mental capacities to change when puberty arrives, and likewise, though not in so radical a way, we expect continual changes through childhood. We see the child developing and are persuaded that human powers are all present by our twenties. But at that point we cease to believe in development. We think we are complete, and do not expect subsequent years to bring us new insights or understanding. Nor can we think this if we hold to conventional outlooks. At the same time we know that evolving humanity is growing ever younger and that nowadays human beings do not intrinsically grow older than 27, or at least that physical and corporeal development ends then and has no more to offer. And therefore what contributes to a person's further development must be drawn from the spirit. And what is thus drawn from the spirit unites with our soul.[17]

A time comes in every person's life when we have to take a conscious hand in how we age. In a lecture given at Epiphany 1918, Rudolf Steiner speaks of this as an essential requirement of our era: 'Human beings have to learn to become consciously older with every passing day.' By this he means not only assimilating and integrating our past but intentionally shaping our future. And by such endeavour, we can recognize ourselves as developing beings of spirit and soul.

In the modern era, people really only grasp the fact that they were once young. They do not fully understand the reality of growing older with every passing day. They fail to see that inherited qualities apparent in youth must be complemented by qualities developed in maturity. If we look back to childhood, we can speak of inherited traits and aspects, of what came to us by birth; and likewise, if we consider our ageing, we can speak of the opposite pole, that of death. In relation to birth we may ask what accrued to us from our forefathers as we entered life. But the other question arises—what are we perhaps losing, or what changes in us, as we live toward the future, as we grow older every day? What is it like to consciously experience our daily ageing?

In fact, this is a pressing need of our times. Human beings have to learn to become consciously older with every passing day. If we do so, this means knowing, truly, that we join with spirit beings, in the same way that being born, having inherited traits, means originating from physical beings. But I will speak next time of how exactly these things are connected, of the important inner impulse the human soul needs to assimilate if it is to discover what it so greatly needs for the future, indispensable for fully complementing what modern science presents from its own angle.

And then you will see why the new Isis myth can come to stand beside the old Osiris myth, and why both together are necessary for modern people. Ancient Egyptian words inscribed on the statue at Sais—'I am the universe, I am the past, the present, the future; no mortal has yet raised my veil'—are no longer sufficient, are now too limiting for the human soul. Into them must resound other words: 'I am the human being. I am the past, the present and the future. Every mortal should raise my veil.'[18]

> Before we examine the reciprocal relationship of young and old, and the effects of education on our maturity and old age, we will first recapitulate the characteristic phases of life as summarized by Rudolf Steiner in his lecture on 28 February 1907. Just a few weeks before this, he spoke in Berlin about the 'Education of the Child in the Light of Spiritual Science',[19] developing there an initial approach toward a new form of pedagogy, and describing how education and teaching must take their lead from the child's developmental stages. The following passage is concerned with the right or wrong ways in which we pass through earlier phases of life, and with how this will come to affect us in old age.

Around the age of 35 lies a mid-point in life, a moment regarded as extremely important in all eras when people knew something of spiritual science. By the age of 21 we have drawn from our three bodies what lies within us as predisposition, and by the age of 27 have drawn from our environment what it could make freely available. And now we begin to work independently upon our bodies, first consolidating our astral nature. Previously we were obliged to learn through and from our environment, but now our judgement acquires a certain traction for our surroundings. Prior to this, it is advisable for us not to shut ourselves off too strictly from our surroundings through our judgement of the world. Only around the age of 35 ought we to consolidate our views. And then the astral body becomes more and more dense. Whereas we were only practising previously, receiving influences, we may now exert an influence. Our judgement begins to have some significance for the world around us. Now, at the point when we can try to help do things on the world's behalf, we start to place our own judgement on the scales. The journeyman becomes a counsellor, and others can start to take note of our opinions.

At the age of 35 our experiences can start to become a kind of wisdom. At this age a time has arrived that is also marked in physical life by the fact that our astral and etheric bodies withdraw from the world. Up to the age of 21, and beyond, the astral body acts in the I, in the blood and nervous system. There it exerts a growing, consolidating effect, giving us in this respect a certain solidity. What properly crystallizes in our world of feeling and thought we can harmonize, and bring to expression in courage and mental exertion. We can therefore regard this period also as a time when the circulation and nervous systems develop, and this period concludes around the age of 35, when the etheric body withdraws more from its activity in the outward, physical body. Characteristically, from this midpoint onward, we slowly cease growing but instead consolidate, start to lay down fat, and our muscles gain strength. This is due only to the etheric body starting to withdraw, its powers now released from their work upon the physical body. It incorporates itself instead into what we have developed inwardly, and we develop wisdom. This is why the ancients knew that the counsel of a person in public life can only be of any significance once the etheric body withdraws from the physical. Only at that point can a person embark upon public life, only then can their capacities serve the state.

From the age of 35 a person increasingly withdraws into their inward life. If we look at such a person they will no longer display the expectancy and yearnings of youth. Instead, though, we can experience their views and judgements as carrying weight in public life. At the same time we can observe how the forces and capacities connected with the etheric body—such as memory—start to decline. And then, toward 50 or so, we arrive at the years when the physical principle also withdraws from us, with increasing calcium deposits and slackening of tissues. The physical principle unites increasingly with the etheric principle, and what has settled in bones, muscles, blood and nerves begins to develop a life of its own. A person becomes increasingly spiritual, though this must be sustained and supported by the right kind of education in childhood, which also nourishes the astral body. In the absence of any youthful joy, the astral body is deprived of what now needs to imprint itself into the denser etheric body. And in the absence of this, the potency of inner life cannot develop, and instead a person will become 'childish' in their later years. People who do not absorb fresh vigour in their youth, begin to wither. It is extremely important to observe this, especially also in regard to spiritual science.

The best time to develop spiritual capacities is around the age of 35, when powers are released that otherwise work within the body. They become available then, and we can work with them. It is therefore especially propitious if a person's karma enables them to embark on esoteric development at not too late a stage. We cannot turn inward as long as we are still involved in directing our capacities outwards.

And therefore we should see the period around 35 as a culmination. During the first half of life everything develops regularly and rhythmically, but in the second half stages are no longer so clearly defined. Spiritual science does describe them, but they are less precise.

Only now do we start to work toward the future. What a person elaborates within them in later years will in the future become organ- and body-creating, and will also later become co-creative in the wide cosmos. In future something will be present that we can already observe during the first half of life. This kind of classification may have a somewhat laboured feeling, especially for young people, but if you really absorb the teachings of spiritual science you will no longer find it to be so. Studying human life from a higher vantage point, you will see that this way of considering human life actually leads us to make proper, practical use of it. We need to practise the resignation of waiting until we have the organs we need in order to work rightly in whatever sphere of activity we seek.[20]

Interdependency of youth and age

During his public campaign for the threefold social organism, which preceded the foundation of the first Stuttgart Waldorf School in September 1919, Rudolf Steiner gave lectures in which he addressed the social question from many different angles. In Zurich, on 4 February 1919, he spoke of the fundamental importance for social cohesion of the relationship between young and old. In recent times, says Steiner, one could perceive in this realm the development of a 'profoundly inward social impulse', a symptom for future forms of intergenerational social community.

In earlier times, all self-knowledge, all introspection was far easier, relatively speaking, than it is now. And—not just in the minds of certain groups concerned with wealth and poverty, or from any other doctrinal position—this is because a profoundly inward social impulse is emerging. Nowadays we tend to overlook the fact that all of human life involves a continual ripening. Inwardly authentic people such as Goethe felt this ongoing ripening. Into advanced old age Goethe wanted to go on learning, knowing that, however elderly, he was not yet complete as a person. He looked back to his youth, to the prime of his life, to everything that had happened to him in youth and in his prime, and saw it all as preparation for the experiences of his riper age. People nowadays very rarely think like this, especially not when they think about their place in society. By 20, already, everyone wants to have joined a corporation and be in a position to voice their—as people say—'democratic' views. They are unable to acknowledge the value of a sense of expectancy, of experience accruing as we ripen toward old age. This simply doesn't figure in their outlook. And that is one thing we need to relearn—that all of life brings its gifts and not only the first two or three decades.

Then there is another thing to learn. Besides our awareness of ourselves in the world, we see others, at different ages; especially we see children being born and embarking upon life. In the way humanity has evolved on earth, much that once revealed itself naturally in the human soul can now only be acquired through enormous exertion, through the endeavour to acquire supersensible knowledge or at least to gain true knowledge of life. Just as people in general are shut off from many things that intrinsically belong to them, so this is true of children too. Children are excluded not only from knowledge of what they will experience when they grow up and become elderly, but also from a great deal that once revealed itself to people who lived in a more ancient, instinctive, atavistic clairvoyance. Thus there is something that, from the cradle to the grave, remains hidden from us as long as we only seek knowledge within ourselves. This is one of the defining characteristics of our consciousness soul age. We can strive for a clarity of awareness, yet much in the field this clarity seeks to illumine remains concealed. This is the very singular thing about our era. As children we enter the world; there is something we possess that is important for the world, for humanity's co-existence, for historical understanding. But we cannot discern it if we make do with ourselves—not as child, as man, as woman, not as an old man or woman. Yet it can be perceived by other means. It can be perceived if a mature human soul finely tuned through spiritual discernment—the soul of a man, of a woman, of an old man or woman—looks upon the child and senses there is something revealed there which the child at present cannot perceive themselves, and will never perceive if they are left to themselves, not even by the time they die. It can however be perceived within another's soul, by the old person who looks back upon this child. Here you have something that can manifest by virtue of the child, though not within the child themselves, and not in the man or woman this child will grow into, even by the time they die, but in the other who gazes lovingly upon the infant from the perspective of advanced old age.

I make particular reference to this because, in such an aspect of our age you can find the weaving and working of a social impulse of the very broadest scope. It is, surely, a profound social impetus if life is imbued with something fruitful by virtue of the elderly learning something from the very youngest, of connecting and uniting with them for the highest purposes: not just some random connection between one person and another, but specifically between the elderly and the youngest infant.

This social co-existence points us to the inmost spirit and meaning of our time. [...] In the social and socialist discourses of our era, try to awaken a deeper social sense, a deeper mutual understanding between people, and then, in the social realm also, you will be fulfilling a living task drawn from anthroposophically oriented spiritual science.[21]

> Even years after founding the Waldorf School, Rudolf Steiner did not tire of pointing to the importance of a vibrant school experience for children, particular in relation to their later development and personality. In a lecture of 22 April 1923, he put it like this: 'We must educate in a way that enables people to grow old.' Only strong roots will bear fruit in old age.

When you grow old what do you have to do? If we lack understanding of human nature, we can have no true idea of what it means to be imbued with certain impulses as a child, acquiring them therefore at the only age when this can happen. At this period only was I able to implant these impulses in the soft, pliable child's organism that I still possessed then, with its plastic-musical receptivity. In later life I have a harder body: not necessarily in physical terms but tending toward the sclerotic in its soul-corporeal nature. What education gave me does not grow old at all. It is not too true to say that it does. However old we become, we are still inwardly possessed of the same child being that was ours between, say, the age of 10 and 15. We always bear this within us. But it must be flexible and pliable enough that it can still use this old brain, overlaid by a bald head, as it once used my softer brain in childhood. And if education did not happen in this way, then the enormous gulf opens between age and youth that we can observe today, which so many think is unbridgeable. People often turn things on their head, saying that young people don't understand the old because the old do not know how to be young with youth. This isn't true at all. None of it is. In fact the young expect the old to use their old bodily nature in the right way. Looking at the elderly, young people see something quite different from what they have, and this gives rise also to a natural reverence for the old. Youth sees that it can gain something from age that it cannot acquire from itself yet—but only if age knows how to use its bald head properly, in its own way, just as the child lives with its full head of hair. This is vital. We have to educate in a way that enables people to grow old. Humanity today is suffering from the fact that children and adolescents cannot see, in the elderly, people who have grown old in the right way. In the perception of the young, old people still have children's heads on their shoulders, no different from them! Because of deficiencies in education, people cannot rightly use their elderly bodies and so stay childish, immature. Having a child's head on your shoulders in old age is a very apt way of putting it: during life such a person does not take hold of their whole organism but works only with the head, which is what the child or young person should work with. And so young people say, we can't learn anything from them! They know no more than we do, their heads are just as childish. So it is not a matter of age not being youthful enough nowadays, but of remaining far too childish. This is what makes things so difficult. With the best will in the world, therefore, people have turned things upside down in their appraisal of this generational gulf.[22]

In the end, young people do not wish to be left to their own devices but want to find their place alongside the old. But they should find this place in two ways: firstly by seeing what comes from age as something other than they possess, which they cannot find within themselves, and secondly as something they recognize that they need, that they must introduce into their own souls.

In this respect, life in our society has led to conditions that I would like to characterize as follows. People so often say that the elderly should retain the freshness of youth in order to get along well with the young. But nowadays—and of course present company excepted—the elderly are *too* youthful. Or in other words, people do not know how to grow old in the right way. They do not know how to integrate their soul and spirit into the body that has aged over the course of life, how to grow into it. People keep introducing into the old body the same things they did as children already, or at least as young people. But it doesn't fit any more, the bodily clothing no longer fits. And the lack of accord with the young is not due to a failure of the old to get along with them, because of growing too elderly, but on the contrary, the lack of accord with the young is because they have not grown properly into maturity, and thus become of true value in age. Youth wants elders who have grown fully into age, not childish elders, with childish heads. In contact with the elderly, young people today say, 'They're no different from us. They have learned more but they don't know more than we do. They haven't used their ageing to ripen but have stayed like us.' Youth wants age to be rightly old.

But what this necessitates, for a sound social order, is an educational practice that enables seeds planted during schooling to grow onward into the most advanced age, to bear fruit. I gave instances of this. We have to be able to unfold the right living forces in the right way for each phase of life; we have to know how to grow old. If age knows how to grow properly old it actually remains fresh and vigorous, whereas, if I have grown grey and wrinkly yet still have a child's head on my shoulders, I have nothing to tell young people, nothing to give them more than they already have themselves.[23]

> A misapprehension of youthfulness, embodied in the failure to develop soul-spiritually as one ages, and the possibility of counteracting this through education, contrasts, in the passage below, with the other side of the same materialistic coin: sluggishness or lethargy of soul leads to premature ageing. To combat this sort of aridity, it is important to remain open and receptive throughout life. To remain young in the sense of interested and able to learn, Steiner says on 29 January 1912, in Kassel, makes it possible to pursue the anthroposophic path of schooling.

If you only apply sufficient inner willpower, you can transform your character. We have to learn to feel that an immortal principle holds sway both within ourselves and others. An anthroposophist becomes one by virtue of remaining open and receptive throughout life, even when hair turns grey. And this sense of always being able to progress will transform our whole mental outlook as it is at present, our whole culture.

Materialism makes people prematurely old. Thirty years ago, children looked different from today. Nowadays you already see ten- or twelve-year-old children who strike you as elderly. Human beings have become too 'clever' prematurely, too precocious [...].

It is incredibly important for us always to be able to remain young, irrespective of the age of our physical body. And this is the vitally important task of anthroposophy: to bring the world the rejuvenation it needs. We need to advance beyond the banality of sensory life alone. The aim of our group meetings must be to acknowledge soul and spirit in practice. We can gain mastery over outward existence, and the knowledge that this is so must increasingly fill us.[24]

> We are born with a deep yearning for all spirit. Parents and teachers sense this when they feel the trusting gaze of young children upon them. But if this desire meets with no response, bitter disappointment emerges, especially in adolescence. On 11 March 1923, in Dornach, Rudolf Steiner spoke of the far-reaching consequences of this disappointment, which leads to lack of understanding between young and old. He paints a telling and vivid picture of this condition of the thirsting soul.

And then a curious condition arises when the soul experiences something, but cannot express it, because this is not a conscious experience, though nevertheless present. The soul experiences something that we can describe as follows. When, after puberty, a sleeping person enters the world of spirit, and the world of archangels opens before them, they feel this archangelic world and yet no thoughts are spun from it into their soul, nor from their soul to this world of archangels. And the soul then returns on awakening to their physical body, with this terrible sense of lack or loss.

This is a condition that has arisen for a majority of human

beings since the last third of the nineteenth century. In the unconscious, underlying people's conscious mind, is something that makes them unconsciously awaken and say, 'We have been born into a world that does not enable us rightly to enter into spiritual existence while we sleep.' The souls who experience this state might put it like this: 'As children, we were taken up into a human world whose words closed us off from the spirit, and failed us.' All this lives in the subliminal feelings which young people often harbour toward older ones. That is the spiritual aspect of feelings that manifest in the youth movement.

What do young people want from the old? They cannot express it for their minds tend to be held back rather than opened by what they receive as inheritance from the older generation in the form of education. They can't put it into words, but in the vaguest obscurity of their inner soul life they feel this: As a child I have to find my way into what older generations have given me. These older generations do have to educate me, but they deny me the opportunity of connecting, communicating, with the world of spirit as I need to.

To the same degree that materialism will continue to spread in all areas of life—in science, art and religion—youth will not be able to get along with age. And this is because youth feels age denies it the idealism of language, the real meaning in words that point toward a spiritual life. The materialism of civilization sunders youth from age. And the real source of misunderstanding between them is the way language, eaten away by materialism, calls forth an unhealthy condition in young people's sleeping soul life.[25]

The following day, in speaking again of the human being's relationship with the world of spirit, Steiner described how we must understand the human being from within, as it were, out of the realm of spirit and soul. He emphasized the inner will activity that is needed to do this, which leads to a tangible experience of spirit. What he means becomes apparent in his account of the angelic beings of the hierarchies. And he continues by saying that without this self-invoked power of initiative the human being is at risk of degenerating into a 'spiritual automaton', who must be calmed and placated by analgesics and sedatives. He finds this kind of dampening of inner activity also in the mechanistic pictures of cinema, which really run counter to true imaginative experience.

It is not only necessary that we form a right relationship again with the archangeloi in the realm of language—as I described yesterday—but also that we develop a more intensive relationship with the archai, the primal powers, by activating the will in the more vigorous way that is needed for understanding spiritual science. Then a form of knowledge and perception will become evident that is quite different from the one people are nowadays accustomed to, and with which they are inculcated. And that is what people shy away from so much. To study spiritual science requires will development. The concepts given in the science of the spirit, these ideas, have to be assimilated by a will that develops inner activity. People don't care for this. They prefer to let the will alone, and allow knowledge to unroll before them, to receive it visually without having to make an effort, letting the brain reverberate with these perceptions so that thoughts also run by themselves. People today like it best if you present a kind of film to them instead of lectures, something they do not need to grapple with in thinking—something they can give themselves up to, letting everything pass before their gaze. Then it

impinges on the eyes, stimulates pictures that print themselves in turn on the brain, and, when this has been done
enough times and become firmly imprinted, well then one has
absorbed whatever it is. But when this occurs one becomes a
real automaton, in spiritual terms. There is no need to actively
transform what is presented to the mind, it is just lodged in us.
We become a spiritual automaton. Then, for instance, there is
no need to enquire into the human organism, for to do so
certainly requires inner activity. We will never understand
human nature if we do not approach it with inner activity, and
when we do not, likewise, assimilate ideas such as those I
elaborated today. Though I suppose it would be possible,
without inner activity, to try out the effect of antipyrine on the
human organism. You can try it out, and need not understand
anything about the human being; you can just observe its
effects outwardly, empirically instead, and this can become
imprinted by sufficient repetition—and then you can write a
prescription for it. But in this way, without developing insight
into human nature, you become a spiritual automaton. Much
of modern life runs along these lines.

But the times are prompting us to inner activity again, to
the development of will. And this is what youth wants of age.
Youth wants age to offer it something again that will enable it
to have the right converse with the archangeloi; and also to
provide an education that enables it to form the right
relationship with the archai. Young people know they must
give themselves up to the education of their elders until they
themselves come of age. But in this education lies a trend
toward the inactive, filmic quality I described.[26]

Practising mindfulness is seen as wholesome in our hectic
era. Since time immemorial, the quest for stillness, reflec-

tion and meditation have been regarded as effective paths toward self-knowledge and understanding of the world. Rudolf Steiner emphasizes, though, that reverent devotion should not be blind but must go hand-in-hand with a healthy sense of self. But when reverence is properly developed in childhood, it transforms in our later years into a potent faculty.

Reverence and devotion teach the soul to move from dark desires and instincts, from life's drives and passions, toward moral ideals. We can sow this reverence in the soul as a seed; and it will flourish and blossom.

If we observe life without preconceptions, we can see this in another instance. It is clear, wherever we look, that human life follows an ascending and then a descending trajectory. In childhood and youth development is in ascent, then remains still for a while, before a declining process begins later in life. In a sense we can say that the descending line of development at the end of life is a reverse of what developed in childhood and youth. And yet, in a curious and singular way, the qualities assimilated in childhood and youth become evident again in later life. To a true, careful observation of life, it is apparent that the seed of much well-guided reverence planted in childhood blossoms in old age. This reverence reappears in old age as the power to act in life. As the opposite of the reverence cultivated in youth, strength to be active in life appears later on. A youth spent without reverence, without a properly guided devotion of the will, properly guided feelings of love, will pass into a maturity that is weak and powerless. Intrinsically, therefore, a developing soul can and should be encompassed by such reverence. [...]

Love is part of reverence, and humility or devotion is its other aspect. Devotion and love are similar in this respect, that, if we possess such a feeling at all, we can be devoted to more than one unknown person or thing at the same time. The sense of devotion can be intensified without having to be divided as a finite quantity, however many different creatures or beings we feel it for. Since these two qualities, love and devotion, do not have to be divided, there is no need for the I, which should be a unity, to lose and fragment itself when feeling love and devotion for one and then another unknown thing or person. And love and devotion are therefore the right guides toward higher things we do not yet know, and lead the soul from the rational soul to the consciousness soul. Whereas overcoming anger educates the sentient soul to the sense of truth and striving for truth of our rational soul, reverence educates our consciousness soul. By cultivating reverence, educating the consciousness soul to reverence, we acquire ever more knowledge, ever richer insight. But such reverence must be governed by a self-awareness that does not shy away from the light of thinking. If we let love stream from us, by its own virtue love allows us to bring our being with us. When we incline in devotion, likewise, we may bring our self with us by virtue of this devotion. We may lose ourselves in love and devotion, but do not have to. That is the important thing. And in particular we should not forget this when the impulse of reverence is cultivated in education. We should not inculcate blind, unconscious devotion. Its cultivation must go hand-in-hand with a healthy sense of self.[27]

> It is a matter therefore—and it's worth emphasizing this again—of growing old in the right way. As Steiner comments in his lecture of 22 December 1909, the ripeness of age is a 'boon' to the world. Old people with this quality emanate an inner maturity that has a benevolent effect on others.

Reverence in the first half of life transforms in the second half into a very particular quality. All of us have no doubt heard of individuals who have something like a benevolent effect on those around them simply by the way they are. They do not need to say anything in particular, but only have to be present. It is as if the whole mode and manner of their being emanates something invisible and communicates itself to other souls. Their whole manner has a wholesome and enlivening effect on their surroundings. To what do such people owe this power to act beneficially on those around them through their inner qualities? It is because the first half of their life was graced by reverence, because they experienced this mood of reverence to a great degree. Reverence in the first half of life transforms into the power to emanate an invisible blessing and boon later on.[28]

> The close connection between childhood and age was something Steiner often reiterated specifically in relation to blessing. A decade later, when involved in his pedagogical work, he explained in lectures how praying in childhood can transform in later life into the power to bless.

Things such as this, that I have often emphasized, are no longer in people's awareness—for instance the power to bless in old age, and the importance of this. The blessing an old person can give is of a different quality from that of someone in middle age. People have no sense of this any more, and it is because they no longer know that we have to fold our hands in prayer in childhood if we are to give true blessing in old age. Being able to bless in old age depends on folding our hands in prayer in childhood. In soul terms, blessing and praying are connected in the same way as grey heads and children's heads. This inner transformation is something hard for modern people to recognize or experience, but it must become part of our experience again. People need to regain insight into the different metamorphoses that occur throughout life.[29]

Certainly we can say, as a picture, that hands which have learned to pray in childhood will in later life possess the gift of reaching out to bless another. This is to put it metaphorically, yet it is a true reflection of the fact that seeds planted in childhood work on into the whole of our later life.[30]

Let us imagine a very old person speaking to younger ones, to children for instance; and his words or exhortations just roll off them like water off a duck's back, mean nothing to them. And then imagine someone else whose words to children have a quite different effect. His words flow naturally into their souls. If you were now to study the origin of this capacity to speak to children's souls, this blessed power of an old man or woman—and people do not study these things, because they so rarely consider the whole human being, unable to keep their observation still and steady enough— then sometimes you must trace it back into early infancy. This is beyond the scope of people's observation nowadays, but it is what anthroposophy must do. So you trace this back and you find that a person whose words in old age carry a blessing that resonates in young people, learned to pray in childhood. To encapsulate this in a picture: hands folded in prayer in childhood become hands that bless in old age.[31]

Ageing as a Developmental Process

All life is subject to the laws of growth and decline, and this is implicit both in our individual ageing and in the larger spans of human history. The incisive changes that occurred at the beginning of the twentieth century, with the catastrophic war, were attentively observed by Rudolf Steiner. These changes were a wake-up call to understand historical forces as such. Those familiar with the idea of repeated lives on earth—reincarnation—can glimpse the deeper significance that historical ageing processes, encompassing humanity as a whole, have for each individual and their development. Before we examine the transformations associated with every human biography, we will first consider the greater rhythm of humanity's evolution. Here we are concerned also with insight into how, in each new historical era, humanity attains a higher level of development.

The second and more extensive part of this chapter will then turn to the phenomena of ageing in individual life, considered from the point of view of inner transformative processes. Thus we will, at last, look at some very familiar symptoms of ageing, beginning with the weariness—connected with a transformation—that can begin in the middle of life. Here the soul and spirit start to release themselves from their close connection with the physical body.

This is followed by a nuanced account of changes affecting the power of memory. We can become increasingly forgetful as we age, and Steiner sees this not only a loss but also as a new quality in our perception of the past: 'hidden and slumbering powers of memory awaken'[32] and give us a broader overview of our life, a new and sometimes astonishingly clear perception of childhood and youth. Then he goes on to consider the opposite process, that of forgetting, dealing extensively with its inner significance. He speaks of the misery that tormenting thoughts can bring and the 'blessing of forgetting'. This theme is one that confronts many who work in geriatric care and psychiatry: a whole generation of the elderly still carry unassimilated war memories in them, and this can come to expression in infinitely painful ways on their path toward death. In recent years, with an awareness of 'emotional intelligence', people have come to see that a good connection between heart and head is one of the most important attributes for psychological health. Steiner, ahead of his time here, describes the interplay of heart and head, emphasizing the importance of 'heart knowledge', and seeing in it a means to prevent sclerotic tendencies in the brain which could lead to dementia.

Ageing throughout history

In the often-cited lecture of October 1918, widely known under the title 'What the Angel Does in our Astral Body', Rudolf Steiner stresses the importance of people gaining understanding of historical development, saying this is the only way to become a true contemporary. Here he also explains that humanity as a whole, like the individual, is subject to laws of growth and decline—an insight to which too little attention is given in modern views of history.

A great deal happens in evolution, and people, especially nowadays, are obliged to gain real understanding of evolutionary processes and occurrences, in which they too are involved.

Everyone knows that they must attend to their own

development and not just the outer circumstances around them. Consider this for a moment, in very rough and ready terms: the outward, sense-perceptible realities occurring now surround people who are five, ten, twenty, thirty, fifty or seventy years old; but no reasonable person will expect that, at all these different ages, a person will have the same relationship and response to these outward occurrences. Human development itself will affect how we are to respond and relate to our outer surroundings. Everyone will accept this in respect of an individual human being. But just as an individual is subject to very specific development, and possesses different powers and faculties as a child, in middle age, or as an old person, so humanity likewise continually develops different powers. And we are sleeping through history, really, if we do not acknowledge that humanity is essentially different in the twentieth century from the fifteenth, and still more so from how it was at the time of Golgotha or before that. One of the greatest deficiencies and confusions arises today because people dismiss what I have just said, thinking one can regard the human being or humanity in very abstract and general terms, with no need to acknowledge the evolution through which humanity passes.[33]

> In 1917 Rudolf Steiner gave eight lectures that dealt with the question of freedom and historical imperative. In the passage reproduced here he explains that history is marked by processes of growth and decline: growth processes arrive at their limits, and transformation processes become necessary. Sometimes a quite new historical impulse is needed, and cannot be derived from what has preceded it. In a telling example, Rudolf Steiner describes how abstract thinking associated with preconceived notions can distort a true view of history.

We have to acknowledge this fully: that while evolution, the course of history, progresses in a way that can be compared to a growing tree, this tree ceases to grow when the leaves have reached their fullest extent, the furthest periphery, and then it starts to die. A particular sum of historical occurrences is rooted, to continue the metaphor, in the last third of the eighteenth century, and I will speak of them more specifically tomorrow. These are joined by other influences over the course of the nineteenth century and so on. But these historical events have their span and outermost spread, reach their limits. Such limits are not in fact like those of a tree or plant that ceases to grow any further at its periphery, but a new root of historical occurrences must begin. In the most eminent sense we have been living for decades now in a period when new historical events of this kind must arise from direct intuitions. In fact people can easily succumb to illusions about history. To return to our image, a plant whose inner laws allow it to grow to a certain expanse could be artificially extended by attaching threads to its outermost twigs and hanging paper leaves on these threads. Then an illusory continuance of the tree could be created.

And there *are* such threads in respect of historical events. Though a different mode of historical occurrence should by now have arisen, the old one has been artificially extended. In terms of historical development, these threads are human preconceptions, human love of comfort, which prefers to continue and extend what has actually long since died. Certain people sit down at the end of these dead threads— that is, at the outermost ends of human preconceptions and prejudices—and are often regarded as real, important 'historical figures'. And others have no idea of the degree to which these figures hang at the end of such threads of human prejudice. One of the most important tasks of our time is to form a clear view of how many figures regarded as 'great' today in fact dangle from these threads of human prejudice.[34]

> Next there follows a detailed account of how human soul qualities change from one cultural epoch to another. Each era has its own tasks to fulfil, and alternation between earthly and cosmic existence enables us to prepare for new tasks. This leads to an ongoing process of evolution and maturation in which the whole of humanity is involved, and which cannot be halted despite opposing tendencies.

As you know—and we have often discussed this, with much about it in the lecture cycles—we divide humanity's evolution into certain long aeons which we call Saturn, Sun, Moon and so on; then also shorter periods to which we refer as the Lemurian, Atlantean and our own post-Atlantean times. And then within these smaller periods, which are nevertheless enormously long, we speak of cultural epochs in this post-Atlantean period: those of ancient India, ancient Persia, the Egypto-Chaldean epoch, the Graeco-Roman epoch and our own present fifth post-Atlantean period.

We use these designations because, in its passage through earthly evolution, humanity undergoes essential changes—in this case especially in soul nature and soul qualities. These periods are characteristic of very real evolutionary changes therefore. And now let us speak of the smallest of such epochs. In such a span of time, humanity needs to pass through experiences that bring it joy, suffering, understanding, and from which it must also draw will impulses for its deeds and so forth. In each epoch quite specific tasks arise that differ from Egypto-Chaldean to Graeco-Roman times, and are different again in our own.

These changing tasks in successive cultural eras related to certain human qualities and characteristics, in particular those we will consider today, can only be properly grasped if we try to recognize the nature of experiences that arise from the whole of human life and inform outward historical occurrences. Ordinary history considers only outward events, and our time's materialistic outlook confines itself to them. But these outward historical events of human beings on the physical plane, which encompass after all only a part of the whole of human life—which unfolds not only between birth and death but also between death and rebirth—cannot give us a full sense of the nature of the successive epochs. You see, what actually occurs always also involves a reciprocal interplay with forces coming from the realm in which the human being lives between death and rebirth, which descend and engage with the forces that human beings develop here on the physical plane. There is always an interplay at work between forces which people unfold after death and those that they develop here on the physical plane.

Back in the fourth post-Atlantean epoch, and throughout that whole time, people were, you can say, kept in a kind of unconscious condition about certain things. And a great deal that people were kept in the dark about during the fourth, Graeco-Roman era, must increasingly come to conscious awareness in people of the fifth post-Atlantean period. This fifth post-Atlantean epoch will be one in which much of what could previously remain inaccessible must come to consciousness in human souls.

Such things evolve with a certain spiritual lawfulness, a certain spiritual necessity. By nature the human race is predisposed to develop particular faculties of insight, and also particular will forces, at a specific period. Humanity will become ripe for certain things in the fifth post-Atlantean epoch as it became ripe for other things in earlier epochs. It will become mature enough for them. But one thing which humanity will be ripe enough to acquire in this fifth post-Atlantean epoch appears particularly paradoxical to modern people, and this is because public opinion nowadays tends toward the very opposite, or seeks to direct people toward the very opposite. Yet this will do no good. The spiritual forces that are, let's say, inoculated into humanity over the course of the fifth post-Atlantean epoch will be stronger than what certain people wish, or what public opinion holds to.[35]

Transformation processes in the human soul

As we grow older all kinds of infirmities announce themselves, symptoms that our body is wearing out, hardening and becoming ever less flexible. We only become aware of our organs when something is wrong with them. The body tires and grows sclerotic in a long and gradual process, and we only slowly sense that this harbours a deeper meaning. But when we grow tired in old age, and our outer life seems to be fading away, we can begin to sense our inner life more strongly. If we are attentive, our organism now appears to us as an artwork that originated in cosmic forces. But this knowledge of the structure of our organism and our inherent connection with the whole cosmos only really dawns on us after death, when we work at developing a new body. In a lecture he gave in 1916, Steiner described these matters in much detail, and the knowledge that can be gained in the midst of increasing, age-related weariness.

By the very experience of living we grow tired, worn out. It is always so—we tire and grow weary. But the redress for this weariness through sleep which strengthens us to be conscious once more—though, to be accurate, it is not so much sleep itself as the rest we get by sleeping that restores us—is only a partial redress. For we know of course that life slowly wears us out, that we become older, and that our powers slowly dwindle. We become tired in a more general sense. And once we are older, we know that sleep will never completely restore us. We could ponder this differently, though. We could ask why the gods allow us to grow weary. What is the purpose of it? You see, the fact that we grow tired, that we are gradually worn out, gives us something, signifies really a very great deal for our whole life. But to understand this we have to see the concept of tiredness in a much broader sense than we usually do. We have to reflect deeply on this concept of tiredness.

The best way to get an idea of this is the following. If I were to ask you what you know about the inside of your head, you might say you know most about it when you get a headache. When you have a headache you're aware of the inside of your head, whereas the rest of the time you live in blissful ignorance of it. We feel or sense our organs when they are not working properly, and this gives us a kind of feeling knowledge about them. Life is such that we only really become aware of the physical body when something is wrong with it. We really have only a general feeling or sense of the body, and this grows stronger when something is not right. A mere sense or feeling does not give us much insight. But anyone who has had a severe headache knows something about the inside of their head, an inner knowledge, not like that of the anatomist who knows only its vascular system and so forth. But you see, as we grow ever wearier during life, this sense or feeling of our interior, our spatial interior, arises increasingly in the body.

As we age we grow wearier, and increasingly we are afflicted by infirmities. And therefore our life involves this process of gradually becoming more aware of our physical being, of learning to feel and sense it. As it hardens for us, or, let us say, intrudes more into us, we learn to sense and feel it. Because this happens so gradually, it remains a background feeling. But we could experience how strong it really is if—and forgive this banal example but it does convey what I mean—we could feel the youthful flourish of health one moment, like a healthy, lively child, and the next could feel the frailty of an 80- or 85-year-old. Then certainly we would experience this more strongly. But because it happens so slowly we do not notice it so much—this feeling of being inwoven into the physical body, this feeling of weariness. This developing weariness is a real process that is not there at all to begin with, for children are so full of vitality. Gradually a note of weariness starts to resound, starts to emerge and slowly drowns out the vitality. As we grow more weary, though this may still be a quiet inner murmur, something does actually arise within us. Our life here in the physical world offers us, you see, only the external aspect of profound, significant, lofty secrets. The fact that a quiet weariness accompanies us in life and grows, is the external aspect of something that is being woven within us, wondrously woven out of pure wisdom, a whole tissue of pure wisdom. As our life declines and we grow tired, and learn to sense ourselves inwardly, a subtle knowledge is inwoven into us of the wondrous structure of our organs, our inner organs. Our heart teaches us what it is to grow tired, but this tiredness signifies that a knowledge is being woven into us of how a heart is built up and formed out of the whole cosmos. Our stomach gives us a sense of weariness—and we tire it chiefly by spoiling it with the food we eat—and yet as the stomach grows weary, wisdom is woven into us, a picture of wisdom from the cosmos of how the stomach is formed and structured. A picture arises in us of the noble, wondrous structure of our inner organism, this mighty artwork. And this only comes fully alive when we have laid aside the external aspect of the astral body that is bound up with the earth. And then what fills us and lives in us is life spirit. The wisdom about ourselves, the wondrous structure of our inner organs, now lives within us.[36]

> Another typical ageing phenomenon is the waning of, or, more accurately, the changes to memory. Various aspects of this will be addressed below.
>
> Firstly, general memory loss. This belongs to the natural ageing process, and yet it would be mistaken to regard weakening memory in age only in terms of loss. We can say, rather, that the nature of our awareness, and how we engage with memories, changes over the course of life. In childhood, and far into middle age, a focused and factual kind of knowledge tends to predominate, with a memory to which we can have recourse at any time. In older years, some things are forgotten, but at the same time vivid, pictorial memories can emerge from soul depths, offering an overview of the past. These pictorial powers can be schooled, and if we have practised living thinking we now gain a future orientation through beholding the past.

Is there anyone whose memory does not decline when they grow older? This is a universal and much-regretted phenomenon—the waning and loss of memory and other faculties. The powers of memory we were equipped with out of the store of gifts received at birth now become depleted or exhausted. This will happen however healthy a life we may have led. And although there are various outward means to improve this loss, these innate powers do inevitably decline and become exhausted.

But if we inwardly and actively take hold of what spiritual science can give us, and if we acquire habits of thought and modes of thinking other than the customary ones, we will notice that powers that were once those of memory still wane when we grow old, but are replaced by something that is a far better kind of memory. Out of the soul's spiritual depths emerges what we can call a beholding of the past events of life. In the same way we have been used to looking upon spatial things, we gradually instead learn to look upon temporal things. The powers that memory does not otherwise develop, because it usually has a reserve of them in the body itself, remain hidden until we grow old, and then these slumbering, hidden powers of memory are drawn forth from the soul as powers to behold the past. If we properly live with spiritual science during our life, we develop in ourselves something that replaces our ordinary acquired faculty of memory; and this means that someone who truly engages with spiritual science in a living way remains capable of beholding the past, and also of gaining from the past powers of future orientation, far longer than someone who does not wish to engage with spiritual science. If we discern the finer nuances of such things, we can see how memory becomes something different but no less faithful. In fact, this emerging faculty appears truer to us than the memory innate in us through our physical forces.[37]

> The nature of our memory can also however be considered from a quite different angle. Here we offer a longer passage in which Rudolf Steiner illumines forgetting from an

anthroposophic perspective, and finds unexpectedly positive aspects in it. On 2 November 1908, as part of a lecture series on spiritual anthropology, Steiner spoke about the process of forgetting, finding it necessary to develop the full scope of its importance from the opposite process, that of remembering. How do memories arise? What forces are involved in it? From memory's mode of action he derives insights into forgetting also, seeing it as a necessary dynamic that releases new powers. He also shows that what we forget is not lost but that in fact, through forgetting, impressions and thoughts about our experiences release themselves from their original source in an object or circumstance, and thereby develop a germinal power that works upon the etheric body.

Today we will embark on spiritual-scientific studies that show us how the knowledge we acquire through the anthroposophic worldview can give us insights into life in the broadest sense. Besides developing greater understanding of mundane reality through such knowledge, we also gain broad, wide-ranging insights as we trace life beyond death into the time unfolding for us then between death and a new birth. But spiritual science can be of great benefit precisely for ordinary daily life, solving various riddles and showing us how, if you like, we can cope with life. [...]

The word 'forget' is one that conceals many mysteries; it of course designates the opposite of retention of a particular idea, thought or impression. No doubt you have all had some dismal experience of what this word represents. You have probably all suffered the agony of being unable to recall some idea or impression because it has vanished from your memory. You may then also have wondered why forgetting has to form part of our experience of life.

Only insight into esoteric realities can help us understand such a thing. As you know, memory or recall is connected with what we call the human etheric body. We can therefore assume that the opposite of remembering—forgetting—will likewise have something to do with the etheric body. It may be justified to ask whether any purpose is served by the fact that we can forget things we have once had in our mind. Or must we instead—as so often happens—accept the negative characterization of forgetting as a deficiency of the human soul, our inability to keep everything in mind at once? We will only gain insight into forgetting if we call to mind the significance of its opposite, the importance and nature of memory.

When we say that memory is connected with the etheric body, we also have to ask why it acquires this role of retaining impressions and ideas. After all, a plant has an ether body, and there it has a substantially different function. We have often discussed the fact that in contrast to a mere stone the whole materiality of a plant we see before us is permeated by its ether body. In the plant the ether body is the principle of life in the strict sense, and then also that of repetition. If a plant were subject only to the activity of the ether body, then the leaf principle would simply keep repeating from the root upwards. It is due to the ether body that parts of a living entity keep replicating anew, for it always seeks to keep producing the same thing. Something like this also occurs of course in reproduction, the producing of one's own species, and this is largely dependent on the ether body's activity. [...]

What is this due to? It is due to the fact that in every instance the plant's ether body possesses a certain intrinsic lawfulness, closed off from outer influence and developing from seed to seed: a certain scope that cannot be exceeded.

The human ether body is different. Besides the part of it used for growth, for the same kind of development that in a sense encompasses us as it does the plant, there is another part of the ether body, you can say, that exists freely and has no prior use unless we teach children all sorts of things in educating them, incorporating into the human soul all manner of things which this free part of the ether body makes use of and assimilates. In other words, there really is a part of the human ether body in us that nature does not use. We retain this and do not use it for growth, do not apply it to natural, biological development, but retain it within us as something intrinsically free by means of which we can assimilate the ideas and images which approach us through education.

This assimilation of ideas occurs initially however by virtue of the fact that we receive impressions. We must always receive impressions since all education is also based on impressions and on collaboration between the etheric and astral bodies. To receive impressions, you see, we need the astral body. But to retain an impression so that it does not fade again, the etheric body is needed. The activity of the etheric body is necessary for retaining even the least, apparently most insignificant memory. For instance, if you look at something, you need the astral body. But to retain it after turning your head away, you need the etheric body. The astral body is involved in looking at things, but the etheric body is necessary for retaining the image of it. Though very limited activity of the etheric body retains images in this way, and though it really only comes into its own in relation to lasting habits, inclinations, changes to temperament and so on, nevertheless, this is where it is needed. To retain even a simple idea in our head the etheric body has to be present, since all retention of ideas is in a sense based on memory.

Through educative impressions, through mental development, we incorporate all kinds of things into the free part of our etheric body, and must now ask whether this free part remains of no importance whatever for growth and development. That is not so. The older we become—not so much in younger years—all the educative impressions incorporated into our etheric body participate in the whole life of the human body, also inwardly. You can best understand the nature of this participation if I tell you something that is not usually considered in ordinary life. People think that soul qualities generally have little significance for human life. But the following can happen: someone falls ill simply because of being exposed to adverse climatic conditions. Now we have to picture hypothetically that we can be ill under two types of condition: firstly in a state where we do not have much to assimilate in the free part of our ether body. Let's assume that a person is lethargic, and the outer world makes little impression on them, that they have put great obstacles in the way of others' educational efforts—that things have gone in one ear and out the other. A person like this will not have the same means of recovery as someone else who possesses a lively, active sensibility and has absorbed a great deal in their youth, assimilated a great deal, thus taking very good care of the free part of their etheric body. Practitioners of mainstream medicine, of course, still have a way to go before they can ascertain why greater obstacles to the process of recovery are apparent in one person than in the other. This free part of the ether body, in which manifold impressions have engendered dynamism, comes to the fore here, and its inner mobility participates in the process of recovery. In numerous instances people owe their rapid or painless recovery to the fact that, in their youth, they diligently assimilated the impressions offered to them. Here you see the effect of the spirit on the body! Trying to cure someone who passes through life with dull sensibility is a very different matter from doing the same for someone whose free part of the ether body is not sluggish and lethargic, but has remained active. Empirical evidence of this can be ascertained simply by observing the world with open eyes and seeing the different ways in which mentally lazy and mentally active people respond to illness.

So you can see that the ether body is something quite different in people than in plants. The plant lacks this free aspect of the ether body which allows us to develop. Basically all human development depends on us having this free aspect. If you compare the beans of a millennia ago with those of today, you will see that the difference between them—though there is one—will be very small, and that basically they have remained the same. But compare Europeans at the time of Charlemagne with Europeans today. Why do people today have very different ideas and feelings? It is because they have always possessed a free aspect of their ether body which enabled them to assimilate things and transform their nature. This is all true in general. But now let us consider how all that we have described actually functions in detail.

Let us take the example of someone who, having received an impression, is unable to erase it from their memory again. It would be a strange thing to imagine that everything that has ever made an impression on you from childhood on should be present in your mind every day of your life, from morning through to evening. As you know, all this is only present to your awareness for a certain period after death, where it serves its proper purpose. But during life we forget things. All of you have not only forgotten countless things that you experienced in childhood, but also a great deal of what happened to you last year, and no doubt also some of what happened yesterday. A notion that has disappeared from your memory, which you have 'forgotten', has not however vanished from your entire spiritual organism, the record and pattern of your being. This certainly isn't the case. If you saw a rose yesterday and have now forgotten it, the image of the rose is still present in you, as are all the other impressions you absorbed—even if they have been forgotten as far as your immediate awareness is concerned.

Now there is really an enormous difference between an idea or picture while you remember it and the same idea when it has disappeared from your memory. So let us consider an image formed in response to an external impression, which is now living in our awareness. Then let us cast our eye of soul on the way it gradually disappears, is gradually forgotten. It is still present, though, within our whole spiritual organism. What is it doing there? What is this 'forgotten image' preoccupied with? It has its own very important role. You see, it only begins to work upon this free part of the ether body which I described, and to render this free part of the ether body of use to us once it has been forgotten. It is as if this image or idea has only then been properly assimilated. As long as we make use of it in order to know something with its aid, it is not working inwardly on the free mobility, on the organization of the free part of the ether body. The moment it fades and is forgotten it starts to work. And so we can say that ongoing work is continually underway within the free part of our etheric body. And what is it that undertakes this work? The labourers are our forgotten ideas. That is the great blessing of forgetting! As long as an idea or image sticks in your mind, you relate it to an object. If you observe a rose and retain the memory of it, you relate the rose image to the external rose, so that the image is bound to the external object and is obliged to send out its inner energy towards it. But the moment you forget the image, it is inwardly released and starts to develop germinal powers that work inwardly upon your etheric body. Our forgotten notions therefore have major significance for us. A plant cannot forget nor, of course, can it receive impressions. Simply because it uses up all its ether body for the purposes of growth, it would be unable to forget, having no unused remainder. Even if ideas could enter it, a plant would have nothing with which to develop them.

But everything that happens does so in lawful necessity. Wherever something is present that needs to develop but is not supported in its development, an obstacle to development is created. Everything in an organism that is not incorporated into development becomes a hindrance to development. [...]

The same is true of mental impressions. Someone who, say, could receive impressions but had to retain them continually in their mind, would soon be likely to reach a point where the part of the ether body that should be nourished by forgotten notions would receive too little of such sustenance and would then hamper development like a paralysed limb, instead of furthering it. This is also why it is injurious for us to lie awake at night and fail to get impressions out of our mind due to worry and anxiety. If we could forget them they would become beneficial agents working upon our ether body. This shows vividly that forgetting is a blessing, at the same time highlighting the importance of not compulsively clinging to some notion or other but instead learning to

forget it. It is extremely injurious to a person's health if they
cannot forget certain things.[38]

> Closely bound up with faculties of memory is the way in
> which we assimilate and imbibe knowledge. Of significance
> here is the account, in passages on humanity's 'juvenes-
> cence' (p. 22ff., 111), of the temporal limits to our physical
> developmental capacity, since this has an impact on our
> ability to learn and remember. Rudolf Steiner distinguishes
> here between head knowledge and heart knowledge. The
> former, based on the intellect alone, is limited since the
> human head can only develop during youth, whereas heart
> knowledge endures in the soul through the mutual interplay
> of heart and head. The related concept of 'emotional intel-
> ligence' has become an accepted idea in recent decades.
> Careful cultivation of the child's sensibility is the best pro-
> phylaxis against premature ageing. Steiner's comments here
> have an important connection with the increase in dementia
> rates in our time.

People nowadays completely overlook how things were in
former times. Our conventional history is really a kind of *fable
convenue*, an agreed fable—but we will not dwell on that
today. In former times people were brought up differently. In
early education, much more consideration was given to the
life of feeling and sensibility. Our purely intellectual life has
only emerged in the past four or five hundred years, and fails
to acknowledge that human beings have many different
facets. The intellect is easily developed and educated but it
does not, unfortunately, continue so throughout life, especially not in our present evolutionary cycle. It is bound up
with the human head, and the head only retains its capacity to
develop until the age of 28 at the most. Our lives last three
times the length of the period during which our head can

develop. In our youth, certainly, we can keep developing intellectually, but only until roughly the age of 28. The rest of our organism continues developing throughout life, and also continues to ask something of us. What is given to people today is only head knowledge, not heart knowledge. When I say 'heart knowledge' I mean something that speaks to the whole organism, whereas head knowledge speaks only to the head, intellectually. Now you see, the head has to stand in continual mutual interplay with the heart, also in moral and psychological terms. But this cannot happen nowadays since we give our children so little for their heart, or if you like for the whole of the rest of their organism, only nourishing the head. By the time a person reaches the age of 35, they have nothing but head knowledge or a recall, a memory, of the head knowledge they have assimilated. They recall what they have acquired in purely intellectual terms. Ask yourselves this: is modern education capable of allowing us to step back feelingly, lovingly into what we absorbed in our youth, so that we really still have something of worth from what we were taught, and so that we can refresh it within us and draw upon it? But this capacity to draw sustenance from our education, not only recall it, must become the ideal of spiritual science. Nowadays people don't even do that: they take their exams and then forget what they 'crammed' for. Let us suppose they do remember something of what they were taught, do they do so with gladness, as if looking back to a paradisal condition? When you think of your school days, does it seem to you as if you are returning to the fresh morning of your life, and that, now by virtue of growing older, what you received through schooling is transformed into something fresh and new? Did you assimilate things in a way that allows you not only to recall them but transform them, make them new?

People's inner content of soul will be filled with life if spiritual-scientific principles renew our whole education system, our whole culture. When this happens then the effects of premature ageing will grow ever rarer in humanity. If you trace the course of humanity's evolution, you will find that, prior to the fifteenth century, the oldest in society were not so 'old' as young people are today. Sclerotic symptoms of decline are increasing to a terrible degree.[39]

> The knowledge we absorb should be able to develop further over the course of our life. It is generally accepted today that education does not end once we have finished school or college. Over a century ago, Rudolf Steiner emphasized that knowledge must undergo a continual process of transformation. We should be open enough to keep learning the lessons which life can teach us, 'for otherwise life ceases to have value'. If, when we're old, we judge something in the same way as we did when we were younger, then the intervening life we have lived can be seen as 'worthless'. It has not really brought any benefits. Steiner illustrates this with the example of youthful emotions that should transform by the time we grow old, so that wisdom emerges from mere knowledge.

It is not actually easy to characterize the meaning of wisdom in just a few words. We develop in wisdom if we allow the experiences we have in life to affect us, learning from what happens, learning how we need to strengthen our powers in one way or another; when we attend to everything that we encounter in life in the sense that, if it should happen again, we will no longer let it disturb us as before but we will know better how to deal with it; and when we succeed in keeping a feeling alive in us that we can always learn from life, from all that we meet in nature and life, not just in the sense of accruing knowledge but by growing ever better as human beings, ever more valuable inwardly. Then whatever we experience will not have occurred in vain but will inwardly enrich us.

Life ceases to have value if decades pass by and we judge what we have experienced from the same perspective as we did when younger. We are furthest removed from wisdom if our life passes like that. Our karma might involve us being angry in our youth, being indignant about one thing or another, disparaging others. But if we cling on to such feelings throughout life, we will have made poor use of it. By contrast, we will have lived our life well if at some point later on we no longer disparage others but view them with understanding, with forgiveness, if we make efforts to understand them. If one of our innate qualities was to get angry about certain things, but later on when we're older we no longer react like this, finding, because of what we learned from life, that our rage has departed and we have grown gentler, then we have used our life to cultivate wisdom. Or if we were materialists in our youth, but later let insights from the world of spirit approach us insofar as the times allow it, then, again, we have used our life to grow wiser. If we close ourselves off from the revelations of the spiritual world, on the other hand, we have not used this life to cultivate wisdom.[40]

Ageing: the Risks and Opportunities

So far we have mainly looked at ageing as a process of development and transformation leading to greater maturity. Now we focus on the polarities inherent in the ageing process: the opportunities it conceals but also the risks of a misguided view of this phase of life. Themes here include health and illness through to pathological developments. It becomes apparent that the transitions between natural and pathological states are fluid.

We are concerned here also with the polarity between youth and old age. Events in childhood often correspond to what happens when we are old. As we saw before, there is a very fruitful reciprocity between childhood and the evening of our lives. Rudolf Steiner suggests that people at opposite ends of life feel a spontaneous interest in each other. But more than this, both stages of life depend on each other for their healthy development. Recent research in the field of gerontology is likewise concerned with such reciprocity, seeing it to be useful not only as part of a maturation process but also as something that enhances resilience and thus health in old age (see also the chapter on 'Modern Gerontology, a Survey', page 213).

Particularly important for 'healthy ageing' are the critical or fruitful moments in life when we can either undergo or miss out on certain experiences. Both premature and delayed development have an effect on the whole course of our biography. To age well, we must have been allowed to be children fully when young. It is important that premature external demands or externally imposed concepts do not 'cool us down' too early if we are to nurture within us a potential that gradually unfolds during the rest of our life (see also the chapter 'Growing Old—a Challenge for Education', p. 169).

The all too limited view of the elderly today tends to emphasize their increasing infirmity. This will be true if we take only physical aspects into account, and therefore perceive only physical processes of decline. Earlier we saw, however, that enriching soul-spiritual processes of transformation arise from the middle of life onward, a theme we will pursue further below by examining certain laws and patterns in human biography. Even the typical illnesses of age can be seen in a different way if we take account also of the spiritual and soul transformations associated with them. It is particularly surprising and illuminating in this context to find how Steiner, already a century ago, described and evaluated dementia. The anthroposophic view of the human being enables us to understand and perhaps also better cope with some of the pathologies arising in old age.

The art of growing old

After the end of the First World War, in relation to the necessary renewal of society and the practical realization of these ideas in the field of education, Steiner repeatedly highlighted the importance of seeking to understand the impulses which souls bring with them at birth. Young children are filled with the longing to preserve a connection with their origins. They hope to meet people during their life who will stimulate and encourage them in a way that will enable them to keep developing, fruitfully, to the end of their life. According to Steiner, they need people who 'have understood how to grow old'. There is a time for everything, and real maturity presupposes that we can wait patiently for each due season—an outlook which, already in Steiner's day, seemed to hold little attraction for many people.

Young people want elders who have grown old in the right way. Wrinkles, white hair and bald heads are not enough if an old person is intrinsically still as young or immature as the young. Youth wants people who have understood how to grow old: who, as they grew older, have increased in wisdom and strength.[41]

In former times, people were young, and grew old in a more natural and self-evident way than today. Nowadays people live in a world, really, in which they cannot be naturally young and old at all. Today people no longer know what it means to be young or old, and that is why they speak so endlessly about education: they want to know how to make youth young in a way that will enable them to become old in a respectable fashion. But they do not have any idea how to achieve this—how to help young people to be properly young and absorb what will later allow them to lead an old age of human dignity.[42]

It is essential that people come to recognize that an impulse must be implanted in infancy that will later enable a person to learn to grow older. Nowadays, people do not understand how to grow old. They know that they get grey hair or—especially common today—go bald prematurely; or other similar signs of ageing. But they do not possess something that they could: a sense of expectancy, hopeful expectancy of what each new year will bring. They do not possess the certainty that each new year will enable them to experience something new that they could not previously have experienced; a new insight or understanding, if only they could make use of it.

Gradually it must become apparent to people at the age of 20, say, that a 30- or 40-year-old will have experienced things they cannot as yet experience. They must learn to wait for insights that only increasing age will bring them. This is a serious matter, which I would like you to consider: please try to think through the full ramifications of what it would mean in society if education enabled people to behold the possibility of future experiences with hopeful expectancy. [...]

Instead, young whippersnappers continually insist on their own view and entitlement. Nowadays people already have a point of view in earliest youth. The idea of waiting in hope and expectancy, the idea that life hides its secrets and these only gradually become apparent, is something unheard of. But it would be very significant if this outlook could be introduced through education. Then people would find the will slowly to release and redeem from enchantment the spell in which their body and destiny are bound.[43]

> In former times, ageing was regarded less as a period of decline only, as it is nowadays, but instead people harboured a mood of expectancy sustained beyond the end of physical life. Since such a feeling was 'naturally given' it inevitably faded over the ages. But it can and should be reawoken through education, by helping each individual kindle the spark of spirit knowledge. The increasing infirmities of age can be set against soul-spiritual maturation. Awakening to the spirit in our time is a matter of individual freedom. In his lecture in Stuttgart on 26 April 1918, Rudolf Steiner speaks of the need to reawaken a mood of expectancy and hope as we look into the future.

Try to imagine the feeling with which people awaited growing older in the past—a feeling very different from the one
prevalent today. It is markedly different from our modern
outlook to have a sense of expectancy about increasing age,
knowing that experiences which cannot come earlier will
then be granted us.

That has changed, but perhaps not in such a crass way as
we normally imagine. In fact, ageing cannot be seen in one
way only, and it is a poverty of thinking in our time that
people regard such matters in black-and-white terms. It is
usually better to see things in a more nuanced way, with the
potential to go in either direction. The spirit does not
announce itself inevitably as we grow older, but if the spark of
it—as spiritual science sees it—has been kindled in the soul,
this will benefit us as we grow older: from the declining body
arises something that makes itself a habitation, especially, in
what we have learned or become acquainted with through
spiritual science. If, in our times, you decline to engage with
the spirit through study—and I don't mean 'study' in the
academic sense, but in a way that everyone can pursue if they
care to, even the simplest soul, for the science of the spirit
could come to popular attention if humanity desires it—then
you will not experience anything much in old age, and will
not know how to value it. Nor will you harbour any particular
expectancy in childhood and youth about growing older in
the future. But it will be different if the spark of spirit
knowledge is implanted in the soul, not any longer as a
natural birthright but through education, so that what for-
merly was given in natural evolution is now instigated by an
evolution in which education takes a hand, in which such
things are imparted to human society. If people properly
understand how spiritual science brings life to the soul, then,

in a conscious way now, a mood can be re-engendered in them that they have something to look forward to when they grow older; that growing older has meaning. As a young whippersnapper of just 20, I would then know that what lives in me will change and be different by the time I am 35. To cultivate this mood is incredibly important for the human soul: a mood that I will call one of expectancy toward life, the intuitive sense that the creativity you experience at work in yourself must in fact be seen as creation out of the spirit.

Do those today who wish to have nothing to do with spirit knowledge seriously regard human creativity—even if they use this term superficially—as a creation out of the spirit? No, in practice not at all. For if they did, they would recognize that there is a meaning in growing old. The whole of human life is a spiritual creation. We do not grow old in vain, the spirit continually comes to expression in us anew. What arises in us and manifests through us, continually displays new aspects. To live with expectancy, to expect something fruitful from growing ever older with each passing year, follows from acknowledging that what surrounds us and is within us is a creation of the spirit. Living in expectancy in this way engenders a mood that must become embedded in all education, that must flow into the whole foundation of educational endeavour. From infancy through to adolescence and beyond, children should gain the sense that as long as they are young the spirit does not yet give them everything, but as they grow older it continually reveals new things that rise up from within them. We need only the impulse that teaches us about the spirit to recognize, and not overlook, what seeks to rise up from the depths of our being and makes growing old meaningful, not meaningless. [. . .]

Let it not be said that spiritual science, if properly understood, is anything abstract, and has no value for practical life. As spiritual science comes to be ever better understood it will have very great practical effects, for it will find its way into people's actual feelings. Its effect will be that people grow up differently, with a different expectancy of what each year of their lives can bring them. Spiritual science contains the most dynamic educational ferment, the most energetic impulses for education. [...]

It is essential, you see, that an outlook connected with what I have now said should gain entry into human sensibility through the science of the spirit. Our time has been led into such dire catastrophe because, in this transitional period when something new seeks to flow into the human soul, people still cling to the old and refuse to take up these new feelings, especially refuse to introduce them into their educational principles. In outer life, proceeding from today's materialistic culture, we often find the very opposite of what the future now so urgently demands of us. Above all, the sense of meaningful development in life is something that should be impressed on young people. And in this respect everyone is still a young person today, for as yet spiritual science is still far from becoming embedded in our culture, and everyone still needs to imbue themselves with the gifts spiritual science can bring to the education of the human soul. We must dispel the belief that we have finished learning and developing by the age of 20 or 25, and then simply need to get on with living, and that life only has a meaning in so far as we apply what we learned when young, or in so far as we enjoy life and so on.

If we examine circumstances today more closely, what has been said can make a very, very deep impression on us. Something that developed by itself once upon a time must in our time be inculcated into human sensibility through education, and this is an outlook, a way of life, founded on expectancy. Oh it is highly significant, you see, if, at the age of 30, a person knows that secrets will gradually be revealed to them by virtue of growing five, or ten years older; if they know they can have this expectation. Please consider what this means if introduced into education. It is something real too. It is a current of reality that comes to expression in us, and in our time has to be cultivated, and only then will be present and appear in us. If we do not attend to it, and do not concern ourselves with it, it will not come into existence. It would be wrong to think that you can avoid growing wiser, that you will fail to receive the secrets that age brings with it simply by disregarding these secrets and this wisdom. The spirit is at work in you. You will all become insightful and inventive! The difference is only that one person absorbs the spirit intentionally while the other—who has decided they are clever enough in their twenties (and in the so-called world of intellect, they may well be so)—dismisses the opportunity to receive something more later in their development. [. . .]

What happens with this spirit, this real spirit that developed by itself in ancient times? Yes indeed, this spirit must atomize. Truly it fragments and is dispersed, evaporates in the spiritual atmosphere, spreads out in the aura of humanity. And this is something that must be impressed on people today, time and time again, though naturally they do not credit it for the simple reason that they think it fantasy so say something like the following: Here we have a young journalist who thinks they are very clever. They know nothing about the spirit, but this spirit attenuates into the aura of humanity, is atomized. The person's spirit is still there nevertheless. The aura of humanity is today entirely impregnated by such atomized spirit. It must be made to cohere again by people precisely through the mood I spoke of. You see we are today very close to the point when a terrible evil must arise if the spirit keeps being atomized in this way, if this process continues. It is an important law of spiritual life that a spirit becomes something quite different from what it was originally if it departs from its bearer. Please take this in a very precise sense: a spirit that departs from its bearer and atomizes, becomes something quite different from what it is if its bearer makes it cohere. It deteriorates in key respects, is worsened, is ahrimanically transformed. And this will result in a terrible spiritual vacuity, a wasteland. This is not yet clear today since we are still at the beginning of developments that can have dire consequences. People will seek for something to preoccupy them since they have allowed the spirit which should have been their preoccupation to atomize. A quest for something without knowing what it is one seeks, is a phenomenon that will become ever more widespread if we do not counteract this evil. Today we already see the first signs of this, as I have mentioned before. [...]

This wasteland will spread to a dreadful extent if humanity does not grasp the need for the kind of mood I have just described. This is what people fail to understand today: life's immediate reality! The principle that what exists is a creation of the living spirit does however require a flexible and mobile capacity of experience. It is to some degree uncomfortable to acknowledge that one is never finished and done with, that one is always developing. Yet that is essential if humanity is to progress in its spiritual evolution.[44]

In the 1921 'Christmas Course' for teachers in Dornach, which focused on 'Healthy Human Development', the seriousness of the task in relation to young people led Steiner to speak once again about age-appropriate development. It is important, he says, to understand human biography in terms of its various developmental stages. The middle phase of life, when we are still flexible and adaptable, is decisive for our maturity in old age. If we do not mature properly, our development can take wrong or even pathological directions.

The account I have given you of inner, moral life, exemplified by a couple of instances, must also certainly be brought to bear at the very outset of our considerations on human nature if we are to arrive at a real art of education and teaching. And this can be done as follows.

If we compare the entirety of the human being in life with the animal, we find that the latter, especially higher animals, possess the skills and aptitudes they need almost from the moment of birth. When it crawls out of the egg, the chick is already fully adapted to its environment and does not need to learn; its organs possess the kind of firm plasticity that each animal requires, depending on its species. This is not true of human beings. We are born helpless and have to develop and acquire skills in particular areas through interaction with our surroundings. That we can do so is due to the most important stage of middle life between childhood and old age. This middle stage, this time of maturation, is the most important of all for human life here on earth. During this phase we adapt our organization to external life by acquiring skills and abilities. We engage with the outer world in experiential reciprocity. This middle phase, during which our organs still possess their pliable plasticity, is one actually entirely lacking in animals. At birth, animals already possess the kind of nature we have only in our later years, when our forms become more fixed and their plasticity firmer. If we wish to understand the relationship which animals have to the world, we can only properly do so if we compare them with people in their later years.

We can then ask, though, whether the animal also immediately expresses its soul qualities in a way that equates with that of human old age. That is not the case, since another pole also exists in the animal, which counteracts this inner elderliness—and that is the reproductive capacity. For the human being or creature that bears this reproductive capacity, it has a rejuvenating effect. While the animal develops elderliness in one respect, but has the reproductive capacity flowing into this, it is in a certain way protected from premature senility until it becomes capable of reproduction.

If you are able to observe an animal or animal species without preconceptions, you will discern that at the moment the animal acquires the capacity to reproduce its kind, it has, really, entered upon old age. It is a distinctive quality of human beings that childhood on the one hand, and old age on the other, are situated at the two ends of life, with an intermediate phase of organic plasticity in which we can adapt to the outer world through our relationship with it. In a sense, when this middle phase is properly present in us, human life is as it should be. Given this, people will be children at the right time, and then at the right time cease to be children, will enter into their maturity and, again at the right time, will pass from this phase into that of old age.[45]

> But, as Steiner goes on to make clear, this normal development can be distorted and assume pathological forms. Premature elderliness can lead to an 'animalistic', instinctive clairvoyance.

If we consider this whole biographical trajectory of human life in terms of its temporal phases, this gives us also a point of departure for discerning abnormalities. In certain human individuals we can observe a lack of ability, if I can put it like that, to hold back old age for long enough. I am not thinking at all of the outward signs of age such as grey hair or premature baldness—that is not what I mean; for even a bald head can retain its childlike qualities. I am thinking of the elderliness that manifests more in inward and organic ways, and is only apparent to an inward and intimate kind of observation of life. This is the elderliness of the soul, if we can so express it, which plays into a person's life even when they are outwardly still in the flexible and plastic phase.

The reverse can also happen: a person may be unable to move on from childish things at the due time. Then childishness plays into the middle phase of life: what a person should possess as the inner soul of a child remains present into middle age. This gives rise in human biography to some very curious phenomena that we will now briefly outline.

Normal human life here provides a pattern against which to gauge abnormalities. As we age, our head especially, our head organization, loses its inner mobility, its mobile plasticity. We become stiffer, less plastic as far as our head organization is concerned, as we move toward the end of our life. And all the faculties we acquired in life become more ensouled and more spiritual in old age. But this occurs at the cost of an animalization of our head organization. Physically, we become as the animal is from the beginning, in a sense growing animalized. By virtue of this—if education is properly conducted—we acquire what can still be retained for our remaining years as a soul-spiritual connection with life; in these later years this is purchased at the cost of our soul and spiritual experiences of the world no longer fully entering our organization. The skull is too rigid, its plasticity too solid, and so, in old age, we are more preoccupied with our spirit and soul connections with the outer world. No longer to the same degree as previously do we incorporate our experiences of the outer world into our inner nature. An animalization of our upper organization occurs.

This animalization of our upper organization in age can be displaced into the age of early maturity, in the interior way I suggested. But since a person naturally will always remain human, even if in a sense their head becomes animalized, we do not discern what is described here in any outward characteristics or signs, but only in inner idiosyncrasies of soul. This occurs as follows: if this particular way of connecting with the outer world that pertains to old age arrives too early—and it can even arrive in childhood—it pervades the physical organization since in that period of life plasticity still of course otherwise holds sway; and then the person will have a premature, inner experience of what we experience in a healthy relationship to the outer world if we have known how to grow old at the right time. This experience connects instead with our physical body, is absorbed into the physical organization, giving rise to qualities that grow to resemble animal nature more closely than is the case in normal circumstances.

We can say that animals have the advantage over human beings of a certain natural instinct that connects them with their surroundings more closely than a person usually is connected. This is by no means a legend, but an intrinsic truth, that certain animals sense when natural dangers threaten and withdraw from places of danger. Animals have a certain instinctive, prophetic gift when it comes to their self-preservation. It is also fully accurate to say that animals have a much more intense feeling experience of the course of the seasons. The bird senses the time of year approaching when it must fly south, or, if it is a migrating creature, when it must migrate to other places. Thus animals have an intimate, instinctive relationship to their environment. And if we could see into the motions of animal soul life, we could discern their instinctive wisdom, albeit wrapped in unconsciousness, manifesting as a co-existence with all natural processes.

If, in the way described, a person's life is prematurely affected by elderliness, this instinctive experience of the environment surfaces in the human being, though not exactly as it does in animals, since in us everything is raised into a human quality. Nevertheless a person will develop an instinctive mode of experiencing their surroundings. Everything known today and often rightly—though also often mistakenly—described as lower clairvoyance, as telepathy, teleplasty, telekinesis, abnormalities of this kind, are nothing other than an influx of premature elderliness into an earlier phase of human life and experience. If we experience elderliness at the right time, this is a sound and healthy thing. But if it comes upon us when we are only 20, we become clairvoyant in a lower sense. Here premature elderliness and abnormality manifest not so much in outer signs as inner characteristics. People would gain much deeper insight into this lower type of clairvoyance, manifesting in telepathy, telekinesis and teleplasty—phenomena to which much research has been devoted—if they could recognize that we are faced here with premature inner elderliness.

But then we must progress to a real observation of life. In the present moment we must be able to look beyond what stands before us in space, and interpret it also, acknowl-

edging that idiosyncrasies we can presently observe are due
to an element that ought to come later in life, which plays in
already to an earlier phase.[46]

> A longer meditative passage by Rudolf Steiner ends this
> section. Here, during the last winter of the Great War, he
> once again considers the developmental character of
> maturation and the macrocosmic factors in human evolu-
> tion. Only if we see ourselves as originating in prebirth
> existence can we grasp earthly life as the opportunity for a
> transformation whose fruits can be borne into the realm
> after death. Then we can meet ageing with the necessary
> stance of expectancy, knowing that particular insights will be
> granted us. For this to develop in us, it is important—and a
> factor to be borne in mind in education—that 'the content of
> our head should become the content of our heart'.

Nowadays the dead and the living diverge a good deal in their
outlooks. The soul of someone who has died is certainly
aware that a person quickly develops their head faculties, but
that heart faculties develop more slowly. And if the soul of a
person who has died seeks to express what actually occurs
when swiftly acquired head knowledge works its way into the
slower unfolding of heart knowledge, they will say this: mere
wisdom of the intellect is transformed by the heart's warmth,
or love, that arises within someone. Wisdom in people is
fertilized by love. That is how the dead would put it.

In fact this is a profoundly important law of life. We can
acquire head knowledge quickly; we can know a huge
amount in our time particularly, for science—not scientists
themselves, but science—has advanced a great deal today,
and is rich in content. But this content is not transformed
into heart knowledge; head knowledge remains everywhere
as it is. And this is because people [...] no longer attend to

what develops in life after the age of 27, because they no longer understand how to grow old; or I might also say, how to remain young as they grow old.

Because people fail to maintain their inner vivacity, their heart grows cold: heart warmth does not stream up to the head; love, that should rise from the rest of the human organism, fails to make the head fruitful, and head knowledge remains cold and theoretical. It would not need to remain cold theory, though, for all head knowledge can be transformed into heart knowledge. And that, precisely, is the task of the future: that head knowledge is slowly transformed into heart knowledge. And when this happens, real wonders can occur. [...]

There is no better foundation than modern science, as long as it transforms itself into what can flow toward the human head from the rest of the organism, but now from the spiritual part of the rest of the organism. The wonders that will occur will involve people learning also to feel the rejuvenation of their etheric body, so that modern, materialistic science will become spiritualized. It will be increasingly spiritualized to the degree that people emerge who can demonstrate science's present materialism and the foolishness of this materialistic outlook.

This will be connected with a complete transformation, palpable to anyone who has even a little sense of what is happening today: a complete transformation of education and teaching. No one with open eyes for social, ethical and historical circumstances can hide from themselves the fact that we are very far from being able, as a whole humanity, to—well, if we want to put it in crass terms—bring children up appropriately and especially teach them in the right way. Certainly, we can make children into civil servants, or industrialists, or even priests and so on, but we have little ability to help children to become full human beings, fully rounded people. The times urgently demand that if people are to become full human beings, with a fully rounded and developed soul-spiritual organism, then they must be able to transform what they absorb as children throughout the rest of their lives. Throughout life we must remain fresh and vigorous in a way that allows us to transform what we assimilated when young.

People don't see these things with an open enough mind. What happens to people, really, in their later life? In our youth we learn things—some learn more, others less. There is pride at the fact, isn't there, that illiteracy no longer exists in western Europe? Some learn a great deal, others less, but everyone learns something when young. But what do they do later with what they learned, irrespective of whether they learned much or little? Everything is predisposed to ensure that people only recall what they learned. In what way do people integrate this learning? The human soul is not taught to work in a way that enables head content to become heart content. There is no foundation laid down for this. A lot more water will have to flow under the bridge before what we can give young people—taking only one area, but applicable to all others—becomes something suitable for transforming into real heart knowledge. What must happen for this to come about? Today we have no possibility of giving our children something that could really become heart knowledge. Two conditions are lacking for this, and they can only be brought about by a spiritual science which is truly worthy of the name.

Two conditions are lacking that would give children today something really enlivening and life-enhancing, something that can be a source of joy and dignity throughout life. One of these is that people today, with all the current thinking with which education equips us, can gain no real idea of their relationship with the cosmos. Reflect on everything that children are taught in school about the universe, even the youngest ones. They are compelled to grow up with ideas like this: here is the earth, and it rotates at such and such a speed through space, and apart from the earth there are the sun and planets and fixed stars. And these are described, at most, in terms of a kind of cosmic physics, and no more than that: cosmic mechanics, cosmic physics.

Now is there any connection between astronomy today, in the way it informs what children are taught about the structure of the universe, and actual human beings walking about on the earth? Do these have anything to do with each other? Certainly not! As far as science is concerned, a human being is just a slightly more evolved animal who walks around on the earth, who is born, dies, is buried; then another comes, is born, dies, is buried, and so on. So it goes on from one generation to another. Out in the greater universe things take their course, calculated in purely mathematical terms as a cosmic machinery. But for modern minds what does that cosmic machine have to do with the fact that this rather highly evolved animal is born and dies on the earth? Priests have no wisdom to offer to redress this comfortless outlook. And because they have nothing to offer, they do not concern themselves with this science at all but appeal to faith as to a quite different source.

Well, we do not need to pursue this any further. But there is a deep gulf sundering the statements of atheistic science from the pieties of the various churches, which must inevitably try to sustain the theist element. It was necessary for

earlier views of the universe to be superseded by the one
which has now held sway for a while in human evolution. We
need not look back very far—though people neglect to do
so—and we discover that people still had an awareness then
that, rather than being higher animals who are born and are
buried, they were connected with the starry universe, the
whole cosmos. In their own way, and this was different from
the outlook we must now endeavour to develop, they knew
they were connected with the universe. But this being so,
they had to conceive of the universe also in different terms.

The kind of worldview now taught to children, the
mechanistic view of the cosmos, was inconceivable in the
twelfth and thirteenth centuries. People then looked up to the
stars and planets as we do today, but rather than just making
calculations as modern astronomists do, working out the
orbits of the planets and suchlike, and seeing them as balls
travelling through space, medieval science saw every planet
as the body of a spiritual being. Back then it would have been
blatant nonsense to think that a planet was just a ball of
matter. If you read Thomas Aquinas you will find that he sees
angelic—not English[*]—intelligence in every planet and star.
No one in those times conceived of the kind of astronomy
that has been fabricated nowadays. But in order to progress
in evolution, it was necessary for a while to expel the soul
from the cosmos, and conceive of its skeleton, the mere
machinery of the universe. The worldview that arrived with
Copernicus, Galileo and Kepler was inevitable, but only
fools will regard it as the final valid word on the cosmos. It is a
beginning, but one that needs to evolve further.

The science of the spirit knows some things that conven-

---

[*] In German, 'engelisch' and not 'englisch'.

tional astronomy does not yet know. But it is important that precisely these things that spiritual science knows but external astronomy does not, pass into the common awareness of humanity. Though they may still appear difficult today, these ideas, they will develop into a form that can be taught to children, and will be important and valuable especially for keeping children's souls fresh and alive. But at present we must still discuss these things in difficult concepts. As long as spiritual science is regarded in general as it is today, it will have no opportunity to form these concepts into the kind of ideas needed to make them part of education in childhood.

There is one thing, for instance, that modern astronomy knows nothing about—that as the earth hurtles through space it is actually orbiting too quickly. And because it moves too quickly our heads develop more quickly than would be true if the earth orbited as slowly as would properly correspond to the length of our whole life. The rapidity of our head development is simply connected with the earth's over-rapid passage through the cosmos. Our head keeps pace with the earth's rapidity of movement, while the rest of our organism does not. The rest of our organism withdraws from cosmic occurrences. Our head, whose sphere is an image of the heavens, has to keep pace with the earth's movements in the heavens.

The rest of our organism, which is not created in the image of the whole cosmos, does not accompany this motion, but develops at a slower measure. If our whole organism kept pace with the earth's rapid motion through the cosmos, its development, correspondingly rapid, would mean that we could never grow to be older than 27. That would be the average span of human life. You see, it is true to say that our head is finished and complete by the age of 27, and if it were just a matter of our head, we could die at that age. It is only because the rest of us is tuned to a longer lifespan and goes on nourishing the head continually with its forces after the age of 27, that we can live for as long as we can. The spiritual part of the rest of the human organism supplies its forces to the head. The heart part of us exchanges its forces with the head.

When humanity eventually realizes that it has a dual nature, a head and a heart nature, then it will also acknowledge that the head obeys quite different cosmic laws from the rest of the organism. Then we will once again stand fully within the whole macrocosm, and will inevitably think as follows: I am not just a higher animal on the earth but a being who has been formed out of the whole cosmos; and the earth has appended the rest of my organism to me, which does not at present echo the motions of the cosmos in the way the head accompanies these motions.

Thus, if we do not reflect on human nature in the abstract as modern scientists do, but if we regard it as a picture of duality—as head aspect and heart aspect connected in different ways with the cosmos—then we can learn to place ourselves once more into the universe and be part of it. It is clear to me, and to others too who can judge such things, that if we can warm our thoughts so that when we look upon the human head, we see in it an image of the whole star-sown firmament with its wonders, then into the human soul will flow all kinds of pictures of our human connection with the far-flung, widespread universe. And these pictures will become forms of narrative we do not as yet possess, giving— not abstract but feeling—expression to what we can pour into the hearts of the youngest children. Then their hearts will feel this: I stand here on the earth as a human being, but as human being I am an expression of the whole star-sown cosmos; in me the whole world utters itself. It will become possible to bring up children with the feeling that they are part of the whole cosmos. This is the first condition.

The second is the following. We must try to organize all education and teaching so people can perceive that, while their head is an image of the universe,[47] the rest of their organism withdraws from this universe; and so they can perceive that with this organism they must assimilate the universe, which trickles down as it were like soul rain, so that the cosmos comes to independent existence within the human being here on earth. This too will be a distinctive inner experience. Picture to yourself this twofold human being, whom I will now try to illustrate in this curious form. From the whole cosmos, as people will come to know, the secrets of all the stars enter the human head unconsciously; and this influx, stimulating the forces of the head, is something we must assimilate with the rest of the organism throughout our lives so that we preserve it here on earth, bear it through death and bear it back into the world of spirit. If this becomes part of our living, feeling sensibility, people will know themselves to be twofold in nature, both a head and a heart person. What I am now saying, you see, is connected with the fact that people will learn to solve the riddle of themselves; to say: As I increasingly become a heart person, thus remaining youthful, what my heart gives me allows me to see, as I age, what I learned as a child with my head. The heart looks up toward the head, and will see there an image of the whole starry heavens. But the head will gaze upon the heart and will find there the secrets of the human enigma, will learn to fathom in the heart the true nature of the human being. [. . .]

But as I go on living, as I approach closer to the death that is to bear me into the world of spirit, what I learn with the head will eventually be made fruitful by the love ascending from the rest of the organism, and this head knowledge will change entirely. There is something within me as a human being present only in me as human being. I can live in expectancy. A great deal lies in these words, and it means a very great deal if a person is educated in such a way that they can say, 'I can live in expectancy'. I will grow to be 30, 40, 50, 60, and as I grow older from decade to decade, my ageing brings toward me increasingly something of the secret of the human being. I have something to expect from the very fact of living.

Imagine if this were not merely theoretical but living wisdom, living social wisdom, then the child will be brought up to know, 'I can learn something, but those who teach me have within them something I cannot learn, that I can only acquire by becoming as old as they are and finding it within me. In telling me of this, they give me something that must remain a holy secret for me since I hear it from their mouths but cannot find it in me yet.' Imagine what this would mean in turn for the relationship between young and old: it would create something that has been entirely erased in our time. Imagine that a person would know the sense of expectancy of different phases of life; that they would know: 'I cannot, before I am 40, possess the sum of secrets that take up residence in the soul of a 40-year-old. And if I hear of them, I must receive them as utterance only, and cannot yet know them at first hand.' What a bond of human community would be forged in this way, giving rise to a new solemnity, a new depth in life![48]

Biographical laws

'There is a time for everything.' This Biblical wisdom appears at first glance to be out of date. But increasingly, in the face of our hectic lifestyle, virtues of slowness and mindfulness are being invoked, and it may be apposite to recall that a human life, too, has its own periodicities. Every gardener knows that there are favourable or unfavourable times for sowing seed. The same is true in education, and in the whole of human life. It is not by chance that biographical rhythms are regarded as so important both in Waldorf education and in anthroposophic biography work.

The following lecture excerpts are devoted to particular aspects in the phases of human life, firstly the pattern of seven-year rhythms.

As you will recall [. . .] we identify different periods or phases in every human life [. . .], each lasting roughly seven years. In the first half of life, these phases unfold in a fairly regular fashion. These seven-year phases become less regular in the second or declining period of life. This is so because, in the first half of life, we are in a way recapitulating the regularity of laws and realities of humanity's evolutionary path since primordial times, whereas in the second half of life we are prefiguring something that will only come about in future, not repeating something that has already occurred in the outer world. In the future, therefore, the second half of human life will become much more regular than it is today—ever more and more regular.[49]

> In the first Pedagogical Course (*The Foundations of Human Experience*) which Steiner held in August 1919, immediately before the Waldorf School opened in Stuttgart, he offered prospective teachers fundamental insights into the soul's

metamorphoses through different phases of life. Thus everything that happens in childhood is significant for old age. During life, the soul's inner configuration transforms: changes occur to the ways in which our thinking, feeling and will interrelate. There is a close connection between will and feeling in the fidgety or excited child, but these must be able to separate from each other as we grow up so that, in maturity, a sound connection can be forged between feeling and thinking.

If you observe newborn children, their forms, movements, expressions of life in crying, babbling and so on, you get a picture primarily of the human body. Yet this picture of the human body only comes fully into its own when related to middle age and old age. In middle age our soul nature is more pronounced, in old age, our spiritual nature. [. . .]

If by contrast we observe the expressions of life in someone toward middle age, we can establish a first basis for observing soul nature. This is why someone in middle age can tend, in a sense, to deny their soul nature—can appear either soulless or very full of soul; and this is because our soul qualities reside in the sphere of human freedom, in education too. That many people become very soulless in their middle age does not contradict the fact that these middle years are really ones of soul quality. If you compare the more restless, unconsciously active bodily nature of the child with the more contemplative and calm bodily nature in older years, then you have on the one hand a body manifest as body especially in the child, and a body, in old age, that allows the body as such to recede, that in a sense denies itself as body.

If we apply these observations more to the soul realm, then we will acknowledge that we bear within us thinking perception, feeling and will. Observing the child, the picture of soul qualities the child presents to us is one with a close association between will and feeling. Will and feeling are in a sense fused together in the child. When children fidget or kick, they perform movements that correspond to their immediate feeling in that moment. They are not able to detach these movements from their feelings.

In old age it is of course different: the opposite is true. Now thinking perception and feeling have fused, and will appears to some degree autonomous. Thus human life unfolds inwardly so that feeling, which is first closely bound up with will, gradually detaches itself from will. And this is something we must often consider in education: the release of feeling from will. Then the feeling which has detached itself from will connects instead with thinking perception, with cognition. The later phase of life requires this. We only properly prepare children for later life if we enable feeling to separate itself well from will. Then, at a later age, as man or woman, this released feeling will be able to connect with thinking and cognition, and in this way will be able to meet life's demands. Why do we listen to old people when they tell us the story of their lives? Because, in the course of their life, they have united their personal sensibility with their concepts and ideas. The concepts and ideas of an old person who has really connected their feeling with their thinking perception therefore sound imbued with reality, tangible, personal. By contrast, the concepts and ideas of someone who has not advanced inwardly beyond the phase of early adulthood sound theoretical, abstract, 'scientific'. It is intrinsic to human life that our soul faculties pass through a certain trajectory, the child's feeling will developing gradually into the old person's feeling thought. The scope of human life lies between, and we will only educate children well for this human life if we are able to observe these things from the right psychological perspective. [...][50]

You have to look for the sphere of will and feeling in children also in their senses. This is why we so strongly emphasize that, as well as intellectually educating children we must also continually act upon their will. We must also cultivate will and feeling in everything the child looks at, perceives, for otherwise we really act counter to the child's feeling. Only when someone is in the evening of their life can we speak to them in a way that regards feelings too as having undergone metamorphosis. In an old person, feeling has passed on from feeling will to feeling thinking, or thinking feeling; feeling has changed in nature. Feelings now have a more thought-imbued character, and have dispensed with the restless quality of the will. They now display greater tranquillity. Not until a person has grown old can we say that their feelings have approached the character of concept and ideas.[51]

> In the autumn of 1918, Rudolf Steiner spoke of the laws and patterns in human life, pointing to the connection between biographical and cosmic rhythms. Above all, he explained how every phase of life only acquires its 'sense and meaning' in relation to the others. Not until old age do we become more deeply acquainted with the formative forces that build and develop the body in the first seven years of life. This shows, once again, how youth and age are interrelated, and how a bridge needs building from the one to the other.

During these first seven years, wisdom, of no minor kind, holds sway in the human organism. When children first 'see the light of day' as the expression goes, the brain is as yet fairly undifferentiated. It grows more differentiated over time; and the structures that form within it really correspond, if you study this, to the influences of a wisdom deeper than any wisdom we human beings can consciously summon when we construct machines, say, or pursue scientific studies. What we unconsciously perform after birth is of course not something we can later consciously undertake. Cosmic reason or intelligence holds sway in us then, of the same kind we spoke of when describing the development of speech in a child. Truly, a high cosmic intelligence holds sway in a person during the first seven years of life.

In the second seven-year phase, this cosmic intelligence shifts its focus toward tingeing the human being with everything that leads to sexual maturity. At that stage already it holds sway to a lesser degree. We can put it like this: the wisdom that remains over and is not used inwardly, rises into the head. The head gains something from it, though often some time later! But what the head receives in this way is really only what is left over from its action within our unconscious soul life. And then we continue to develop in further seven-year phases.

Ordinarily people do not nowadays study the whole of so-called 'ordinary' human life, for to do so requires a certain devotion, firstly to the true nature of the human being and then also to the great cosmic laws. But however strange it sounds, what holds sway in infancy, in the first seven years, is not something that can be understood—certainly not as a child, nor as an adolescent, not even in one's twenties when people think they grasp everything about life. It cannot be understood. Only between the age of 56 and 63, roughly, can we come to some small understanding of what happens in childhood if we seek this insight within us, in inner experience. Not until advanced old age do we have the means to gain just a little insight into what holds sway in us in the first seven years of childhood. This is an uncomfortable truth, for people wish to be in full command of all their capacities when scarcely more than young whippersnappers. It is not a pleasant thing to concede that there is something in the world, something even within oneself, that we can only begin to understand toward the end of our fifties. And when it is a matter of understanding what occurs and develops toward puberty, thus between the ages of 7 and 14, we can only gain some insight, some inward, human experience of the kind possible for us, between, roughly, the age of 49 and 56, from around the beginning of our fifties.

It would be good if such truths could find acknowledgement, for they would enable us to learn to understand life, whereas other truths that are ordinarily asserted about human life are governed by what people desire. Unconscious desires play in, but go unnoticed. And then again, what unfolds from puberty to the age of 21 is only available to inner experience—so that we can also form a certain view about it—between the age of 42 and 49; and likewise what happens as we develop between the age of 21 and 28 can only be understood to some degree between the age of 35 and 42. What I say in this regard is based on a real observation of life that must follow when we deepen capacities of spiritual-scientific observation, as opposed to the trivial 'self-knowledge' people speak of today, that is not worthy of the name. I am speaking of real self-knowledge, that is, knowledge of, and insight into, the nature of the human being. And only between 28 and 35, roughly, can we experience something that is understood at the same time as we experience it. In this phase there is a certain equilibrium between understanding and thinking. In the first half of life we can think and conceive of various things; but in order to have an experience of understanding what we think and conceive in the first half of life, we have to wait for the second half of life. [. . .]

It is not for nothing that we live a changing and self-metamorphosing life. We live a life in which every phase of life gains its sense and meaning in relation to the other phases. And this is why we live what is called a normal life—if this is granted us, and we will speak of early deaths tomorrow—through into our sixties and beyond, so that things holding sway in us in the first half of life come to a degree of clarity for us only in the second half of life. [. . .]

In our youth we think, and in older age we understand. [. . .] The wisest person can learn from the infant! And of course, the wisest will be those who do gladly learn from the infant. Though they will not want to be taught by them about morals or suchlike, they can gain infinite wisdom from the young child in relation to cosmic secrets that come to expression then in a way quite different from how they do later in life. The interest holding sway between one soul and the other is greatly enlarged if such matters are not merely abstract theories but when they become the experience of living wisdom.[52]

> In the last year of his life, in Torquay, Rudolf Steiner gave lectures on *True and False Paths in Spiritual Enquiry*. Here, in connection with various states of consciousness and initiate knowledge, he spoke also of the different phases of human life and their close relationship with the starry spheres. Experiences in these spheres are not comparable with sensory experience, but are purely spiritual in nature. Steiner describes how the phases of life correspond to the different planetary spheres. He begins with birth and early infancy in relation to the moon, and ends with Saturn, which relates to

a person's life experiences between 56 and 63. Following
this phase come the 'gift years' which are no longer subject
to these stringent planetary laws.

The ancients, who still knew something of these things, did
not speak of the moon but of the moon sphere, and in what
we call the moon they saw only a point on this sphere's
outermost boundary. This point continually moves, so that
in 28 days we can discern the whole periphery of the moon
sphere. The strength to gaze into what remains as moon
sphere when the earth pales, is one we acquire when inner
human experiences between birth and age 7 become the
power of Inspiration. And when the experiences of the
second phase of life, between second dentition and puberty,
also become the power of Inspiration, then we experience the
sphere of Mercury. [. . .]

We stand with the earth in Mercury, and these Mercury
experiences only become visible to us through the eye we can
develop if we consciously delve back, in vision, into our
earthly experiences between the ages of 7 and 14. At puberty,
passing through the ages from 14 to 21, we live our way into
the Venus sphere. The ancients were by no means dull-
witted. Their dreamlike knowledge taught them a great deal
about these things. The planetary sphere into which we work
our way at puberty they called by the name that is connected
with the love life that begins at this age.

Then, going further, if we look back consciously to what
we experience between the ages of 21 and 42, we find ourselves in the sun sphere. And so you see, if we transform
each phase of life into an inner organ or faculty, it gives us
the strength to broaden our consciousness out into the cosmos, to gradually extend and broaden it. Once again it is

true that we cannot know anything of the sun sphere before we are 42. The beings of Mercury can tell us this for they know it already. We learn this indirectly therefore, through supersensible instruction. But if we are to experience something in the sun sphere within our own awareness, and to experience it in the same way we become familiar with Torquay by walking through it, it is not enough to live from 21 to 42, but we must be older than 42, must be able to look back to that phase from a later one, for its secrets only become apparent in retrospect. And then again, if we can look back on life up to the age of 49, the Mars secrets reveal themselves. The Jupiter secrets are revealed when we look back on our life up to the age of 56. And the very deeply veiled but hugely illuminating Saturn secrets—these secrets which [...] as it were conceal the profoundest depths of the cosmos—reveal themselves if we look back to what happens in us between the ages of 56 and 63. And so you can see from this that the human being is really a small world, a microcosm. [...]

With the earth we stand in interfolding spheres. Seven spheres are interleaved, and during our life we grow into this interfolded totality, are in this way connected with it. Our life from birth to death is unfolded out of our original potential and predisposition, the planetary spheres drawing us onward from birth to death. Once arrived in the Saturn sphere, we have passed through everything that the spheres, or rather the beings of these spheres, can grace us with; and in an esoteric sense we then receive the freely granted, moving life of the universe, which looks back on planetary life from the standpoint of the initiate and which, in a certain respect, can be emancipated from what still acted as imperatives in earlier phases of life.[53]

Typical age-related infirmities: dementia and sclerosis

As we age, we lose capacities and faculties bound up with the body and its organs. We become 'infirm'. Powers of sense perception and memory dwindle and the body hardens. The process is the opposite to that of incarnation in childhood. Rudolf Steiner therefore describes ageing as a natural excarnation process. But what appears outwardly as frailty in the very old can have a quite different inner significance. The elderly are already spiritually in other worlds, and what manifests outwardly as the dulling of faculties is connected, within, with an emancipation of the spirit and soul. This process is first described below in terms of general developments in old age; subsequently we will see how its reaches its fullest extent in age-related dementia.

In a young child, soul and spirit are still in their intrinsically soul and spiritual condition. As we grow, soul and spirit gradually transform into material, bodily nature. Soul and spirit slowly become corporeal. The human being gradually becomes a full image of soul and spirit. It is very important to grasp this idea. If you do, you will no longer think of this two-legged creature that walks about on the earth as 'the human being', but as the image or reflection of the human being; you will see that we are born supersensibly and gradually grow together with the body and create in the body our full image or reflection. Spirit and soul vanish into the body, are ever less manifest in their inherent nature. And so we should develop an idea that is the very opposite of the customary one. We must realize why we have grown to be the age of, say, 20: it is because the spirit has submerged itself in the body, and because this bodily nature is an outward reflection of the spirit. Then we will understand also that as we age a gradual reverse transformation occurs. The body calcifies, silts up, and the spirit returns to a more soul-spiritual condition. But then we are not able to take firm hold of it any more, for it is through the body that it seeks to engage with the physical world and express itself. It becomes ever more independent and only fully manifests after death. Thus it is not true to say that the spirit and soul grow duller as we age, but the opposite: they become ever freer. The materialistic thinker, of course, when told this, will very frequently object that even someone such as Kant, a very intelligent man, grew infirm in old age, and so his spirit and soul cannot have been releasing themselves. But this objection depends on the failure of the materialist to discern or acknowledge how spirit and soul gradually grow into the world of spirit. [. . .]

You see, we have to turn certain ideas on their head to approach the truth. The idea that this world is *maya*, the great illusion, has a lot of validity, for some concepts must be turned upside down. If we take this idea seriously—that we confront a great illusion here in the outer physical world—then we will also be able to credit the fact that, by the time we are 70 and appear frail, the spirit of the outward physical human being is already somewhere else than on the physical plane.[54]

> From 1922 onward, Rudolf Steiner regularly gave lectures to the builders working on the Goetheanum, responding directly to their questions. On 28 June 1923, he spoke of the changes which our mental capacities undergo in the course of life, in this context also describing dementia. Using somewhat drastic terms he described how mental faculties seemingly diminish in old age. The spirit itself, however, cannot be sick or dwindle. It is only the sclerotic body that is no longer sufficient as instrument of the spirit. Growing

childish again in our latter years, says Steiner, is not a misfortune. A person with dementia is instead now inwardly active in a different and far more incisive way, and this can in fact be good fortune.

We develop as human beings. In the general run of human life people do not usually take much note of this, although they do when someone is a child. As we know, a 4-year-old cannot yet write or do sums whereas an 8-year-old may perhaps, and so you can see something has developed. But in later life, once we are 'full-grown adults', we are so proud of ourselves that we no longer admit that we are still developing. In fact we develop throughout life and the way we do is very singular. You see, we develop like this: when the child is very young all development proceeds from the head. After the change of teeth, when you're a bit older, all development proceeds from the chest. That is why we must take such care how children breathe from the age of 7 to 14; that they breathe sufficiently well and so on. This is the age of the older child—though children will no longer let you call them that; you have to address them as a 'young gentleman' or 'young lady'. And then comes puberty, and at that point development proceeds from the limbs. Only when a person becomes sexually mature is the whole of them developing. Then we continue to develop through our twenties, thirties. But you see, when we grow older other things recede in turn. Certain things definitely fade again. Now this doesn't have to be so if one takes care to cultivate mental and spiritual life, but in ordinary human life faculties do dwindle as one grows older. It is in fact anthroposophy's task to ensure that in future people no longer decline when they age, though of course this will be a very long, slow process.

Now there are people of course whose mental faculties decline to a terrible degree. In fact, the spirit itself cannot decline: it is just the body that does. It is interesting actually that it is often precisely very astute people who decline most severely. For example, you will have heard that Kant is held up as a very great and wise figure. But in his dotage he lost all his faculties. In other words, his body declined to such a degree that he could no longer make use of his wise mind and spirit. This is true of many. Very clever people, particularly, can grow to be halfwits in their old age. This is of course again what happens to everyone, just in a more pronounced degree. As we age, it becomes harder to use the physical body, and this is at least partly because very large calcium deposits build up, calcification occurs, especially in our blood vessels. The more that arteriosclerosis develops through calcium deposits, calcium overload, the less we can make use of the physical body. And just as our earlier development started with the head and passed down into the whole of the body, continuing until we are, say, 40, so it dwindles and recedes again in reverse. As we pass from our forties to our fifties, we have to use our chest more again, and in old age we must use our head to a greater degree again. When old, though, we ought not to use our physical head any more but the subtler head, the etheric head up there. Sadly, in Classics-based education, people do not learn to do this, and still less do those who, in recent decades, 'enjoyed' a materialistic, Latin-based education: they will be most likely to succumb to dementia in old age.

In old age we have to return to the level of childhood. There are people in whom this is very apparent. We say that they increasingly lose their mental capacities. And yet the spirit is preserved intact—only the body grows ever weaker.

Ultimately such people can no longer do the things they learned in their earliest childhood. This certainly happens. Let's imagine someone who has grown old and can no longer do things they could do until recently. They can only accomplish what they learned to do as an older child. And eventually, not even that any more. In the end they can only play, and only understand the words they learned as playing infants. In fact there have been people who, in very great old age, only understand the kinds of things that were said to them by their parents or nursemaids in their very earliest infancy. The phrase 'second childhood' is well-founded, for we really do return to childhood in our dotage.

Yet the moment we have spiritual life within us, this is no misfortune at all, but actually fortunate. You see, as a child, we can use our etheric body. When the child shouts and has tantrums or rushes about, it is not the physical body doing this—or only for instance if the child has a stomach ache, but even then the stomach ache has to be transferred to the etheric body and astral body if the stomach ache is to make the child move about. What dances about is not the physical body. But now imagine that we have grown old, and we return to second childhood. Through life we have gradually become accustomed not to romp about, and we use the same etheric body that we used for romping in childhood to better purpose in old age. And so it can become good fortune that we become childlike again.[55]

> In a lecture given to physicians and therapists on 8 October 1920, Rudolf Steiner describes illnesses that correspond to certain phases of life. Every age has its typical illnesses, though their causes often point back to earlier developmental phases. The polarity between youth and age therefore manifests in many illnesses. Childhood diseases

correspond to the phase of physical synthesis and development, during which will-accentuated movement and activity predominate. In old age, calm and tranquillity come to the fore. This latter phase is marked by thinking. The breakdown processes associated with this in the human organism lead to sclerotic conditions.

By pursuing medical research in the field of physiological phenomenology, which I can only touch on here during these brief lectures, we can come to recognize that forces in the human organism, which ought by rights to enter the spirit and soul at the due and proper phase of life, can remain below instead in a person's physical organization. In this case we have a condition of which I spoke to you yesterday: when the normal measure of organizational forces transforms at second dentition, then we have a degree of forces in the organism in a later phase of life that can configure and organize this organism according to its normal form and structure. But if this is not the case, if we transform too few of these forces, then organizing powers remain below and manifest somewhere or other; and then we get new configurations, cancerous ones that I referred to yesterday, and in this way we can trace the pathological process as it develops in a later phase of life. We can then compare this with the nature of childhood diseases, since these of course cannot have the same cause, for they appear in childhood and thus before any such transformation has occurred. But by learning to discern causes of illness later in life, we acquire the ability to observe the cause and sources of childhood diseases. Here in a sense we find the same thing, except now from a different angle. We find here too, when childhood diseases manifest, that there is too much soul-spiritual organizational power in the human organism. Someone who has developed the capacity to observe and perceive such things finds that they manifest with particular vigour when we look at the phenomenon of scarlet fever, or measles, during childhood. Then we observe how what would other-wise function normally in the child's organism, the spirit-soul, starts to rumble, to act to a greater degree than it ought to. The whole course of these diseases becomes compre-hensible the moment we can now actually perceive this rumbling of soul and spirit in the organism as the underlying cause of the illness. And then we are no longer too far dis-tant—and I beg you to take note of my precise words here, for I never claim more than previous deliberations justify, even if some of what is said can only be offered in brief outline, and I always indicate the limits of what is being stated. So I do not say that a definite conclusion can be drawn but that we are no longer too far distant from acknowledging something of very great importance for true diagnosis. If we have reached the point of perceiving the presence of excess organizing force in a pathology in later life that tends toward tumour forma-tion—giving rise therefore to superfluity within an insular organizational pocket—then we are no longer too far distant from stating this: if a later phase of life points us back to earliest childhood, then what manifests in childhood ulti-mately points us back to the time before birth, or let us say, before conception; it points us back to the spirit-soul exis-tence through which the person passed before they were clothed in a physical body. Such a person has simply brought too much spirit and soul with them from their pre-human life, their pre-earthly life, and this superfluity manifests in childhood diseases. In future there will be no alternative but to depart from the unfruitful, materialistic outlooks in which we are stuck currently, especially in the fields of physiology and therapy, and turn to a soul-spiritual outlook. And it will be seen that the findings of spiritual science are not due to the spiritual scientist having too little familiarity with physical research, and being some kind of dilettante in that field (though many who call themselves spiritual researchers are indeed dilettantes, though they shouldn't be). There is no need for spiritual scientists to be unfamiliar with physical research when they pursue their enquiries. On the contrary, they become spiritual scientists by virtue of engaging in it more fully than the ordinary scientist. When they understand phenomena more intently, then these phenomena themselves compel them toward the spirit and soul, especially when we are concerned with illness and pathology.

And then on the other hand, this phrase, 'Perceiving the spirit means destroying the spirit' is really another such absurdity. But this too points us to something that must be acknowledged and fathomed. Just as the phrase, 'Perceiving nature means creating nature' points us to the first phase of childhood, really still to pre-birth existence if we extend it in the right way through seership, so the phrase 'Perceiving the spirit means destroying the spirit' points us to the end of life, to the deadening element in us. It is paradoxical to say this, but you need only keep this phrase in mind—'Perceiving the spirit means destroying the spirit'—and you will find that, although one should not succumb to it, it is nevertheless present as something toward which we are continually drawing close. For someone who does not simply apprehend things naively, as it were, but develops true self-observation, to perceive the spirit implies a seeing, a beholding that is accompanied by continual degrading and destructive processes in the human organism. When we look upon the age of creative synthesis in childhood we see upbuilding processes, though ones with the singularity of dulling our awareness; and this is why we are half asleep and half dreaming in childhood, and consciousness has not yet fully awoken. At that period, this earthly spirituality of ours, this growth activity which suppresses conscious spirituality, pervades and configures us. And at the moment when this power penetrates consciousness it ceases to configure our organism as it previously did. And in the same way that we perceive the upbuilding but consciousness-dulling forces when we look upon childhood, so, in giving ourselves up in vision to developed processes of thinking, we gaze upon breakdown processes, albeit ones fit for rendering our mind and consciousness bright and clear.[56]

> In a lecture to the workers on typical illnesses of different ages, Rudolf Steiner gives a vivid description of the general ailments of age, especially those related to sclerotic tendencies.

What happens in old age, for example? The forces we have then were ones we also possessed in youth, that made our skeletal structure very, very hard, while other parts remained soft. But in old age, when the strength in the bones passes to the rest of the body, first the blood vessels harden, and eventually arteriosclerosis develops. The brain can also calcify. The brain always has to have a little of the process through which furring or calcification arises. If children did not have a little calcareous sand in the head, dispersed, distributed by the pineal gland, they would remain dull-witted, the soul could not engage, for it configures itself into calcium. But later (in age) if too much calcium is deposited, sclerosis results, and once again the soul cannot engage properly if this is too pronounced. Then you get paralysis, cerebral apoplexy or stroke; or otherwise dementia develops since the person can no longer utilize their brain, no longer engage it. But the same is true if calcification occurs elsewhere in the body. When this occurs, we are withdrawn from the forces of the earth. So one can see how we grow into earth forces up to sexual maturity, and then grow back away from the earth again as calcified deposits become ever thicker, so that the soul can no longer properly engage.[57]

> In August 1924, in a lecture to physicians, Rudolf Steiner highlights the causes of sclerotic conditions with great exactitude. He describes how, in such cases, a vigorous, inward-directed spiritual elaboration of soul is instead transposed to an 'external' domain. The astral body and I, which depart from the body during sleep, then absorb excessively strong influences from without. The strong influx of cosmic forces from outside the human being leads to hardening in the body. To withdraw from these forces, the organism sometimes responds with insomnia, itself a pathological form of resistance.

But let us assume this kind of abnormality has arisen within the human organization—that, when we have fallen asleep, the I organization and the astral body root themselves too strongly in the external world, or in other words that they absorb too much of the spirituality of the cosmos outside the human realm. When this happens, these influences become too strong, and every time a person falls asleep they receive these excessive influences, these spiritual influences from without that are too strong in nature. And then they succumb to sclerosis.

The real cause of this condition is that, instead of a person inwardly configuring their whole organism, they receive excessive external effects, specifically when they are asleep. Sometimes, at an older age, when these effects can occur, the human organism employs insomnia to counteract this excessive influence or influx from without. But insomnia is not a solution and cannot be maintained. The consequence is that, when we grow old and yet must sleep, the astral body and I organization that depart from the physical body and etheric body assimilate too much influence from without, and in turn act too strongly on the organism. What do we find when this happens, when, in old age, and obliged to sleep, the departing astral body and I organization take in excessive influences from without and then act too strongly upon the organism? We find, if we introduce lead into this human organism, rendered into an appropriate medicine, that instead of dizziness and faintness occurring, in some circumstances this just holds off the sclerotic forces: the astral forces from without, and the I forces from without—the forces that cause sclerosis—are warded off since then the person also passes through states in which, though they do not fall asleep, the lead drives the astral body and I organization out of the organism yet at the same time holds at bay these excessively strong external influences.[58]

> Rudolf Steiner's discovery that lead can counteract the forces that cause sclerosis was used in the development of a medicine today known as Scleron®. This contains other substances, too, which act similarly to formative forces upon the organism of the older person. Using this anti-arterio-sclerosis medicine as an example, Steiner explained in a lecture to physicians in 1923 how anthroposophic insights into human nature can lead also to the development of remedies and medicines.

When the pathological process rages unhindered, we have to relieve the astral body and I organization of what constitutes this process, and of what they must otherwise undertake. So what must be done if we suffer from sclerosis? Our approach must be to relieve the human astral body of what it has to do for the system of digestion and limbs in an ageing, declining and increasingly sclerotic body. And we can do so by giving lead in a certain dose. This has led to the development of a particular remedy, listed as medicine no. 1 in our medicines index, a remedy against arteriosclerosis. Real insight into the human being makes it immediately apparent that we can substantially address a sclerotic condition by introducing the lead function in an appropriate form into the human being. The proviso here is that we must render the lead active and effective. Simply introducing lead into the organism does not implicitly mean that I have rendered it active there. We can look for further help here from further aspects of a true understanding of the human being.

We gain help from recognizing that we can distinguish between upbuilding and breakdown forces within the organism. The latter are particularly active for instance in sclerosis, where the human organism degenerates. In the head, in the brain, the human organism continually degenerates, for the brain is by its very nature always pervaded by mild sclerosis. Everything therefore depends on our ability to distinguish between breakdown processes and true vitalization processes, processes of synthesis and growth. If we can properly distinguish the two processes from each other, then we first study what sustains upbuilding processes in the human organism in the most eminent sense, which in early childhood is the whole human organism. As yet it is not overburdened by the organs that serve thinking, by the organs that serve the rest of soul activity; it lives initially in the growth organization. And now if we study how the milk function relates to the human organization in childhood, we find this milk function specifically contains the plastic forces the human organism needs in childhood. In a later phase of life we cannot in the same way procure the plastic forces we still require then, which we possess by consuming milk in childhood. Even when very old we still need forces that are plastically active, formative forces which conduct the food we eat into the forms of our organism. Now it turns out that nothing better supports these plastic, active, formative forces in converting the substances we ingest into a form closely aligned with the human organism than eating very small amounts of honey. You see, honey acts upon an old person's organism of metabolism and limbs in a way very similar to how milk acts upon the brain organism of the child, the child quite particularly. This shows us that honey contains special formative forces that we do not isolate by simply subjecting the honey to chemical analysis. We find them only if we actually discern the affinities the human being has, in a fully living context, to the other substances in the universe. It becomes apparent, in a more precise interpretation of these matters, that honey engages the human organism in a way that enables the astral body, primarily, to exert its formative forces; and this formative capacity of honey, these effects it has, can be supported by adding sugar, provided the human organization tolerates this. And so you will find that our first remedy against sclerosis is a preparation—in a manner specially interfolded, functionally interwoven—made from lead, honey and sugar.[59]

Pathological age-related symptoms

In lectures on social renewal given at the beginning of 1920, Rudolf Steiner analysed the turning point which he saw confronting humanity, He again described humanity's 'juvenescence' in relation to its evolutionary capacity. In ancient times it was natural and self-evident that wisdom increased with age, but today this is no longer so. Wisdom only develops and matures if a person can consciously acquire a spiritual outlook as they develop. In the absence of this, pathological developments can occur: people become 'mummified' and lack spiritual responsiveness.

The danger of losing one's mobility of mind and spirit and succumbing to a rigid 'automatism' of thinking, was described by Steiner again six months later, when he warned against becoming 'robotic' in one's thinking in old age because of 'spiritual vacuity'.

I have in the past spoken of this from the most varied angles. Today I wanted to point once again to how the age at which humanity becomes old falls ever earlier. In ancient India, people were not mature till they were in their fifties; in ancient Persia, not until their forties, in the Egyptian-Chaldean era not until the end of their thirties; and in ancient Greece this was at some point in their thirties. We do not mature in this way any more. We just trot on, if we do not enliven ourselves spiritually, but we do not mature. Growing older in ancient eras at the same time signified becoming wiser by virtue of what a person developed in terms of physical corporeality. People growing old today just grow old; they do not become wiser. They become mummified instead. They only grow wiser if they fill this mummified carapace inwardly with something. The Egyptians mummified their dead. Modern people do not need to do this, for they are already walking about as mummies, and only avoid being mummies if they encompass the spirit in its immediate, living presence. Then the mummy is enlivened. But for people today it is necessary to enliven these mummies, otherwise we have these international associations where all sorts of things are uttered by mummified mouths. These associations are called 'parties'.[60]

We can in fact assume that people entertain this idea: that once they are over 50 they lose their thinking capacity! For most of those who have no interest whatsoever in spiritual matters, this is even quite true in a certain sense. I would urge you to examine this carefully, and try to ascertain to what degree people over 50 still produce original, creative thoughts. Usually the thoughts they have are the ones that continue on automatically from earlier years, which have imprinted themselves in their body—and the body just goes on doing what it always has. The body is, after all, an image of thought life; and, clinging to the law of least resistance, people trot along in the same old automatic thoughts. There is scarcely any way to avoid this selfsame mill of thoughts than by absorbing thoughts of a spiritual nature during one's lifetime—thoughts that resemble the thought forces in which we were immersed before we were born. It is true to say that old people will increasingly become robotic if they do not take the trouble to absorb thought forces from the world of spirit. Naturally, we can continue with our automatic thought activity, and it can seem as if we were thinking. But in reality only an automatic action will occur of the organs within which thoughts have taken up residence, into which they have woven themselves, if we do not allow ourselves to be invigorated by that youthful element arising when we absorb thoughts from spiritual science. This absorption of thoughts from spiritual science is not in the least a theoretical matter, but intervenes profoundly in human life.[61]

> In the first medical course, too, which Steiner likewise gave in 1920, he discussed conditions associated with forms of mental immobility, such as the manifestation of delusional thoughts or entrenched stubbornness. Examining these things from a medical perspective, he saw their causes primarily in the diverse organ systems rather than the head, or brain, itself, and believed that therapy must start there.

In fact, the expression 'brain disease' is not strictly speaking correct either. If the term 'mental illness' is completely wrong, that of 'brain disease' is half-wrong, for brain deterioration is in fact always secondary. The primary factor in these diseases never lies in what occurs in our upper system but always only in the lower system. The primary factor lies always in the organs to which the four organ systems belong—the liver, renal, cardiac and pulmonary systems. And when treating someone who tends to forms of madness in which an interest in outward life dies away, leading to inward brooding and delusional ideas, the most important thing of all is to acquire an idea of the nature of their pulmonary process.

In the same way, when confronted with what we might call obstinacy, stubbornness, dogmatism— and thus everything that embodies a kind of immobility of the conceptual system, a rigidity of thinking—it is important to turn one's gaze to the patient's liver process. The malfunction in such a person is, you see, always a matter of their inner, organic chemical reactions.[62]

Changes in the interplay of the different levels of human nature

Earlier we saw how the I of the human being, as eternal spirit, incarnates into three 'sheaths' on the path toward birth. These three forms of corporeality have different tasks and functions. The astral body is the bearer of soul processes, the etheric body the bearer of life processes; and the only tangible sensory aspect of our being is the physical body, through whose resistance human self-awareness kindles. Yet we can experience the *effects* of the physically invisible sheaths. Rudolf Steiner describes this vividly in his lecture of 20 February 1924 to the workers rebuilding the Goetheanum. Here he explains the changes and loosening in the interwoven fabric of these different aspects of our being that can occur in old age, before death, or in pathological states. This account, which encompasses the whole of our human nature, allows us to understand the deeper meaning of ageing-related phenomena. The very long lecture excerpt is here divided by explanatory sub-headings. To begin with, when asked about changes people undergo shortly before death, Steiner starts to speak about the handwriting of old people.

The etheric body loosens

Their handwriting becomes shaky and they can no longer write properly. This brings home to us that they have grown old. Previously they might have written the word 'Lehfeld', say, clearly and distinctly like this (*writes*) but now they write it like this, in shaky script (*writes*). But then, in the last few days before they die, it can happen that they regain their clear and distinctive script, they can suddenly write well again. I have known many people who regained their former, distinct handwriting shortly before they died. It has also been observed in numerous cases—this isn't my own observation but is well substantiated—that people who learned a language when young, perhaps because they were growing up abroad, learned the language, then forgot it again later—so that, we can assume, they would have been unable to converse in this language when they were 40 or 50—suddenly started to speak it again before they died. It emerged again! You see, these are very important phenomena. What is actually happening here? When a person dies, they leave behind, leave to the earth, their physical body, thus a part of their being. This dissolves back into the earth, its form is destroyed. Then I told you that the next aspect of our being, the etheric body, gradually dissolves into the general world ether a few days after death. What remains of the human being still, and passes through the world of spirit, is the astral body, and the I itself. These pass through the spiritual world.

A complete sundering of the different aspects of our being occurs therefore. And someone who has a sense of this can observe, as a person approaches death, how the different members—physical body, etheric body, astral body—separate from each other. Now what is happening if a person's handwriting changes a few days before they die? Well, we do not actually write with our physical body! What do we use to write with? We write with the I! We use the physical body only as the I's instrument when we write. And our I does not grow old. Your I is just as young today as it was when you were born. The I does not age. Nor does the astral body age in the same way as the physical body. But it is the physical body we have to use if we want to write. The physical body must pick up the pen with its hand; and as we age we become ever weaker, and can no longer properly engage our physical body. But besides that, all kinds of deposits form in the physical body itself, and this means that we can no longer make full use of our fingers. We become maladroit, we tremble and make spidery letters instead of clear, firm ones. But as we approach death, the etheric body already starts to loosen itself from the physical body. A loosening occurs. Sometimes this can happen a couple of days before death, or sometimes at the very last moment. This is not to say that we ought not to try to heal a person whom we can see may be going to die soon. What loosens in this way can be reincorporated. As long as a person is still alive, we ought to do everything in our power to cure them. But it is still true to say that the etheric body loosens itself in many people several days before they die.

Now, when the etheric body loosens, a person becomes stronger. That this is true can be seen from another phenomenon. Some people, when insane, develop huge strength, of a quite extraordinary kind. One can be astonished at the strength an insane person of this kind can muster. It is not just that they can attack people around them with far more strength than anyone else could, but they can even, say, easily lift a piece of furniture that no one would otherwise dream of being able to lift. So you can see that something curious happens here, and is out of the ordinary. What is happening here in the case of an insane person? Well, in someone who is mad, the etheric body is always a little loose, or the astral body is loosened. The physical body actually does not render us strong but weak. We have to use the physical body by means of the etheric and astral. The proverbial saying that someone 'has a screw loose' is very accurate, for something is loose indeed. Proverbs often touch on truths since there is a true supersensible instinct at work in folklore. If the etheric body or astral body of an insane person has loosened, and in consequence acquires great strength, then the mad person resembles someone whose etheric body has loosened likewise because they are close to death. And when the latter's etheric strengthens in consequence, their handwriting grows clearer again. Or when, similarly, their astral grows stronger—and this contains everything that we have forgotten—then the person draws forth from this astral body everything they have forgotten and can once again speak a language they knew when young.[63]

The astral body loosens

But now let's take the case you mentioned. Of course I didn't know the man in question, so I don't know how he lived. Did you know him perhaps? If so, you could answer certain questions. Did you know him well? You see, with such a person it is very important to know if he had a wife or someone else nearby—perhaps yourself—who kept telling him how harmful it is to drink alcohol. (This is confirmed.) Well, there we have something straight away that can take us in the right direction. People around him repeatedly urged him not to drink so much, saying that this was wrong and would do him harm. But it went in one ear and out the other, as the saying goes. Again, we have a proverb that is by no means unjustified. It is certainly true that a person's response to certain things may be to let them go in one ear and out the other. Why? Well, it is because the astral body does not deign to hear them. The ear is only the tool of the hearing faculty. The astral body ignores them.

But it can happen that the astral body does hear what is

said but the physical body fails to respond because the person in question is too weak. Let us imagine that our Herr Erbsmehl here told the man himself: 'You're crazy to get drunk the whole time!'—I'm putting this rather strongly, I know—'You can't carry on like that, it's unworthy of you!' And so on, and the man took it all on the chin. That happens in life: people take what they're told on the chin, they accept it all, but they just carry on as before nevertheless. Yet his astral body did retain something of what was said to him. Perhaps you said it to him so insistently and so often that the astral body and the etheric body could not avoid retaining it. While they were embedded in the physical body without hindrance, they registered nothing. But the moment the physical body's condition became such that the etheric body and astral body were loosened, the thought entered this man, via these bodies, that Herr Erbsmehl may have been right after all! 'Perhaps it really is crazy,' he may have thought, 'that I have drunk so much all my life. Now at last,'—you can imagine this happening when things are loosened in this way—'I will do penance!' And now the astral body and the etheric body say: 'Aha, he's not drinking alcohol any more, now he's drinking hot chocolate and sugared water!' Perhaps he would have drunk lemonade too, if there had been any.[64]

The astral body buries itself too deeply in the physical body

For someone who has a grasp of these things they offer proof that all kinds of things can dwell within us that do not necessarily emerge. I told you of an opposite instance on a previous occasion: instead of things staying inside the astral body and etheric body, they go into the physical body too strongly, so that the person in a sense attends too closely to them. The opposite instance was this: a former acquaintance of mine—a very learned gentleman—one day lost his awareness and memory. He no longer knew who he was or what he had been doing. He forgot all his scholarship, forgot everything. He no longer even knew that he was himself. And yet his mind remained clear, he could still reason perfectly well. He went to the railway station, bought a ticket and went on a long journey. He had taken money with him too and could travel a long way. When he arrived at the station specified on the ticket, he bought a new one. He repeated this several times, with no idea what he was doing. His mind was so detached from the rest of him, from who he really was, that everything was done quite sensibly, in the same way that animals act sensibly—as I have often shown with various clear examples, though they do not possess an I. But now he suddenly regained his memory and knew who he was. His erudition also resurfaced in his head, but he found himself in Berlin, in a shelter for homeless people! That is where he had ended up. He had set off from Stuttgart, as was later discovered. He had been in Budapest and other places, without knowing what he was doing. He managed to get back to Stuttgart from Berlin and then one of his family members collected him—they had been terribly worried. But later he took his life, that's how things ended. On the first occasion this emerged in the form of mental absence, and the next time in the form of suicide.

But what is happening in such a case? This man I've been telling you about remains so vividly in my mind's eye that I could paint a picture of him. His eyes looked as if they were sunk deep in his head, and going deeper. Here in front—and I am of course emphasizing what was only hinted at in reality— his nose seemed to bury itself in his body. He spoke in a very curious way too: the way he spoke to you suggested that he was convinced of his words in a way quite different from other people. You had the sense that he was tasting his own words on his tongue and swallowing them because he liked them so much. When he said something it pleased him so much that he wanted to swallow it back into him. And if you contradicted him in any way, he grew very annoyed. He did not display much of this annoyance outwardly but his face contorted. If a wagon rattled by on the road he would wince terribly. And if you told him news of any kind, whether happy or sad, he winced likewise.

This man, you see, had attended too closely, and everything expressed itself immediately in his physical body. In consequence it had become his habit for the astral body to bury itself always very deeply in the physical body; he retained nothing for himself, like your alcoholic, but instead everything buried itself in the physical body—until the physical body had reached a state when his own I also took leave, took flight, for a while.

This is the opposite kind of instance. In the alcoholic we were discussing, the urgings of people around him stayed sitting in his astral body and only emerged when it loosened. In the other case I just mentioned, the astral body settled so deeply within the physical body that the physical body then took on a life of its own.

And so you see that there are signs and indications everywhere in us of how these higher members, these supersensible aspects, are in an intimate connection with our physical body and etheric body. But all this will show you that we can really only understand life if we consider these contexts. They teach us to see that we possess an etheric body, an astral body, an I.[65]

As illustrated in the previous examples, numerous illnesses become comprehensible in terms of the action of the sheaths or members of human nature, especially when their reciprocal interplay changes. In psychogeriatrics, the phenomenon of delusional thoughts is well known. Seemingly threatening figures suddenly appear in patients' rooms, unperceived by others. In his lecture of 31 January 1907, Steiner refers to accounts by the Viennese criminal anthropologist Moritz Benedikt of sensory delusions, or hallucinations, that misled even this sober investigator. Steiner enlarges his observations to encompass the whole human being and interprets pathological developments in the field of psychogeriatrics as disorders of the various supersensible sheaths.

We do not include false perceptions amongst mental illnesses. A book by the Viennese criminal anthropologist Moritz Benedikt has many interesting things to tell us in this regard, despite not being written from a spiritual-scientific perspective. Benedikt gives an account there of his own experiences. He has a partial cataract in his left eye and therefore his vision is somewhat impaired. If he looks in a specific direction in the dark, he sees ghosts of a very particular kind. On one occasion he was so terrified by this that he reached for a weapon. This can be explained as follows: a healthy person is not aware of the eye's inner structures. But if you have visual impairments, you become aware of them as outward reflections, images before you. We can now enlarge this to encompass the whole human being. We are usually completely unaware of our inner organism, only of what is conveyed to us from without. When harmony prevails between above and below, we have no consciousness at all of inner processes within us. But if someone has, say, a sluggish brain that the astral body cannot use, this disorder, suffered by the astral body, manifests outwardly in the same way as the eye disorder. The astral body thus becomes aware of itself through this disturbance: it sees itself as projection, and hopes, desires, wishes appear before the person in outward forms. Insanity, 'disputatious paranoia' and hysteria all belong here—everything that a person cannot bring into harmony with the external world. But the etheric body, too, as the bearer of pictorial thoughts, can suffer from inner abnormalities. If the etheric body is unaware of itself, true pictures of the outer world appear before it. But where, in disorders of the etheric body, pictures are reflected outwards, they become delusional ideas and paranoia. The physical body's task is to establish harmony with our physical surroundings, but if it becomes ill and conscious of itself, imbecility can develop. If the physical body is too heavy so that the astral body cannot master it, cannot emerge from it, what we call dementia occurs.[66]

Old Age and Death

Why do we have to die? A question that can be heard at all ages, sometimes plaintively, sometimes more as a philosophical question. Whatever elicits it, it addresses an existential issue for us. Death processes start at birth, or even during pregnancy. Among other things they are a consequence of metabolic processes. Death processes also however accompany the development of consciousness: every conscious thought is possible only because a death process occurs at the same time in our neurosensory organization, in our neural cells. Waking life consumes the physical and etheric body. According to Rudolf Steiner, we die 'because we live a conscious life'. Ageing and dying therefore not only belong to life but constitute its very worth and dignity.

An anthroposophic, or spiritual-scientific outlook opens up a wealth of perspectives that shed meaningful light on death as a threshold experience. Death is embedded in a higher order, and in cosmic laws. If we take account of this in our preoccupation with death, then suffering can transform into consolation. Knowledge of repeated earthly lives (reincarnation) enables us to place the trajectory of an individual life into a larger context, to understand its origins and to see it in relation to the future. Thus what happens to us in old age acquires its meaning beyond death. Death itself can be understood as having meaningful effects. An early death can certainly seem particularly hard to grasp. Rudolf Steiner's comments point here to the collaboration between human souls and higher spirits of the angelic hierarchies, and to the sway of the laws of destiny, or karma.

The two powers that oppose the intended course of cosmic evolution, Lucifer and Ahriman, act in a way that is very specifically connected with age and death, but also with life after death. Ahrimanic powers show an affinity with processes at work in old age: forces of senescence that seek to harden and condense us, whereas the luciferic powers are associated with rejuvenating and pliable, mobile influences which sometimes, in pathological conditions, lead us back to the stage of childhood and therefore inhibit our maturation.

In the first chapter of this book we saw that the earth too is subject to an ageing process. Life processes can counteract the dying of the earth, comparable to increasing maturity associated with the human ageing process. Here Steiner invites us to examine the human corpse. Before its demise it was pervaded by human spirit, and this is precisely the important thing. Because I forces were active within it, it was 'inoculated' by subtle energies. And with the corpse—as it were in homoeopathic doses—enlivening human forces infuse the earth's dying materiality.

The last section of the present chapter is likewise concerned with the spirit's enlivening power. The dead are only sundered from our earthly conditions if we deny their presence, for then they cannot find access to us. In sleep, in particular, we can enter into contact with them, and hold fruitful dialogue.

Why we die

Our waking life is like dying plant life during winter. Each day we introduce forces of decline into our organism, and we die when they have sufficiently accumulated. The reason for death lies in our consciousness. And we can deduce from this that our conscious waking life, pervaded by the I, consumes our physical and etheric body. We die because we live consciously.[67]

But, seen from the perspective of sleep, the body of an adult, or even of a child from a certain age onward, presents a continual process of decline and degeneration. It is true that destructive forces are deadened each night during sleep by forces of growth, and that what the day destroys the night rejuvenates, but there is always a surfeit of destructive forces. And because of this surfeit we eventually die. Their preponderance accumulates. Each night a preponderance remains, the forces replenished at night are never as great as those that were used up during the day. And so, in ordinary human life, a certain residue of destructive forces remains over, this remainder being added day after day to that already accumulated, leading eventually to natural death in old age as the destructive forces increasingly gain the upper hand.[68]

In the second medical course in 1921, Rudolf Steiner speaks about natural death occurring when the relationship between spirit and body alters in such a way that the spirit, the I, can no longer master or govern physical life processes. The process of dying is therefore closely connected with our I consciousness. We do not understand death if we regard it only as a physical matter, as a cessation of life.

Steiner then speaks very specifically about age-related death, which occurs when the nutritional process can no longer act sufficiently. Then degrading processes outweigh upbuilding ones.

Thus what is initiated from the human head, and from there radiates through the whole organism, is the purely physical process which, at the moment death occurs, pours itself into the whole organism. This moment is actually always present in the human head, or at least emanates from its centre. But it is kept in check, paralysed, by the vitalization process issuing from the rest of the organism. We continually bear within us the forces that also make us die, and we would not be an I if we did not bear them in us. We could only desire to be immortal as a physical human being on earth if we were willing to relinquish our I consciousness. [. . .]

It must be said, though, that the I for as long as possible counteracts the physical process at work within us, the physical process pervading us, but that this counteraction is subject to the described reactive effect. The I counteracts the physical process until the latter grows too strong. This physical process is of the same quality as death always has within the human organism, and as it ultimately manifests in death itself. You see, if the physical process atrophies so that the I cannot govern it any longer, then the I has to sunder itself from the physical body. And this can of course also happen at an early age if an excessive physical action occurs somewhere in the body, and affects other parts of the body; and so we can say that by its nature the human I is intimately bound up with death:

I—death

The most apt way of studying the I is by studying death— but not in that generalized and nebulous way that people usually picture death, which covers a multitude of sins. The way people conceive of death nowadays could equally apply to the destruction of a machine, for they think death is merely cessation. They do not conceive of the real process involved, and so they equate it with something like a mechanical failure. But this is vacuous. We have to get further, to the real facts. Mere cessation of life is not death, but rather it is, for human beings, as I have described it here. [. . .][69]

Now I have to say first of all that, very specifically, human death occurs when our whole inner organization has passed over into the physical in such a way that no nutritional process, no thorough nutritional process, can be initiated any more. This is the death of old age. Death as a consequence of old age is really an incapacity to assimilate substances into the organism any more. This phenomenon has not really been fully observed, and is so little observed because a person usually dies earlier, from other causes, before marasmus or decrepitude arrives in its full-blown state. But it is in fact a failure of food assimilation. The body can no longer undertake proper nutrition: it has become too physical to do so [. . .].[70]

> In the winter of 1906, Steiner gave a lecture entitled 'Understanding Illness and Death'. In examining this theme, he described the I activity that comes to expression during life and in repeated earthly lives in manifold processes of transformation, showing how, contrary to common suppositions, death enables us to understand individual life and why life consumes its own foundations. This self-consuming naturally leads to age-related conditions such as the fading of memory, and failing eyesight or hearing. Steiner summarizes this in the insight that 'death is the root of conscious life'. The starting point for the following passage is the work of the I upon the astral body, and the transformation of drives and desires into moral sensibility.

And so we can say that this astral body always has two aspects: one naturally endowed and another that the I itself has given birth to. We only understand the work of the I if we recognize that we human beings pass through reincarnation, through repeated lives on earth; that, when we are born, we bring with us the fruits and outcomes of former lives on

earth, as it were in four distinct 'bodies', which exist as a
measure of the energy and strength of our life. One person is
born with a great deal of life energy, with vigorous forces for
transforming their astral body. Another will soon lose this
impetus. If one can examine clairvoyantly how the I begins to
work independently on the astral body, mastering desires,
drives and passions by subjecting them to its governance,
then it would be possible to gauge by the degree of energy
that the I has brought with it, how long it will be able to work
upon its transformation—for a given length of time and no
more. And after sexual maturity has arrived, each person has
their own particular measure of this energy, by means of
which one can establish up to what point they will have elaborated from their astral body all the resources accorded
them in this particular life. The life forces a person is able to
transform and purify in their soul become self-sustaining. As
long as the measure suffices, they live at the expense of the
self-sustaining astral body. Once this is exhausted, they no
longer find any courage to transform new drives, or to put it
succinctly, they have no further energy to work upon themselves; and at that point their life-thread snaps. It does so
inevitably at some point, according to the individual measure
accorded each person. The time has then come when the
astral body must draw its forces from the principle of human
life most readily available, from the etheric body. And now
the time arrives when the astral body lives at the expense of
the strength stored in the etheric body, expressed in the fact
that our memory and productive power of imagination
gradually fails.

It has often been said here that the etheric body is the
bearer of the productive pictorial capacity in us, and of
memory, of what we call hope and courage for life. These

feelings, when they become a lasting element, adhere to the etheric body. They are now imbibed by the astral body. And having lived in this way at the expense of the etheric body, and having imbibed from it everything it has to offer, the time comes when the astral body starts to consume the creative powers of the physical body. Once these have been consumed, the physical body's life force fades, the body hardens, the pulse slows. The astral body eventually consumes the vigour of the physical body and once it has done so it is no longer possible for the physical body to be further sustained by the physical principle.

If the astral body succeeds in becoming free and being born into the life and work of the I, then in the second half of life, once the measure of its work has been exhausted, this freed astral body must itself again consume its sheaths in the same way as these were previously formed. Thus is individual life created out of the I.

Here is a metaphor for this process: imagine a piece of wood that you kindle. You could not do so if it did not have the properties it possesses. The flame flickers up from the piece of wood, but it consumes it at the same time. This is the nature of the flame, that it is released from the wood but at the same time consumes what gives rise to it, its own matrix. In the same way the astral body is born thrice, consuming its own foundations like the flame consuming the wood. And individual life becomes possible by virtue of consuming its own foundations again. Death is therefore the root of life, and there could not be any conscious, individual life if death did not exist. We can only grasp and comprehend death by seeking to perceive its source, and therefore we understand life only by perceiving its relationship to death.[71]

If human beings had always known that death is the seed of life, they would not have developed autonomous I-hood, for they would have remained connected with the world of spirit. But death arose in a form that gave them an illusion they were sundered from the spiritual world, and in this way educated us to independent selfhood.[72]

> In reality there is no death. This radical comment was one that Steiner urged upon his audience in the midst of war, in a lecture on the death experience. At the threshold of death the human I awakens, according to Steiner, to its true being, experiencing the victory of the spirit over corporeal nature. Steiner describes this moment as 'the most fulfilling, most consummate event' that we can experience as human beings.

Death is something that, more than anything else, has two totally different aspects. Seen from here, from the physical world, death no doubt has many aspects that are painful and comfortless. But it really is true to say that we only see death from one perspective here, and after death see it from a quite different one: there it becomes the most fulfilling, consummate event that we can experience, a living reality. Whereas here it is proof, brought home fully to our feeling, of the transience and fragility of physical life, death seen from the world of spirit brings us proof that the spirit is always victorious over all that is not spirit, that spirit is invariably life everlasting, an ever-replenished source. It is in fact proof that there is in reality no death, that death is *maya*, illusion. Herein lies the great difference between life that lasts from death to rebirth, and the life here on earth from birth to death.[73]

A long life or an early death

> There were many war dead, many who died far too young.
> Rudolf Steiner frequently spoke of their destiny, and in his
> lecture on 5 September 1915 gave an especially detailed
> account of the meaning of dying young or in old age. Those
> who depart from life early bring something quite different to
> worlds of spirit from those who die after a long life. World
> evolution needs both. An early death can lead to brilliance in
> a next life. A death in old age strengthens the forces that
> serve, in particular, the elaboration of the new physical
> body. In both cases, though, death has an effect upon our
> future destiny and the harmony of the whole universe.

Human beings die at all ages. That goes without saying. But
people are hardly inclined to sense the mystery repeatedly
attendant on this. Yet great mysteries do come to expression
in these most daily occurrences of life. [. . .]

Now it makes an enormous difference, one you can
recognize if you keep in mind what I have just said, whether
we die when very old or in youth, perhaps even as a child. If
we die in youth, our etheric body has not yet grown so young.
[. . .]

You see, to fashion a new life on earth requires a great deal.
If it were left to human wisdom alone to fashion a new life on
earth by itself, nothing much good would come of it, you can
be sure. Imagine for a moment that you yourself, your own
consciousness, had to create the human being's whole physical instrument. Then you would have to be thoroughly
conversant with it, wouldn't you? Yet any familiarity with
external science will show us how much human beings really
know of the composition of their physical body! Between
death and rebirth we can do this to the extent of forming the

physical body in a way that enables this body, right into its finest intricacies, to bring to expression the predisposition created by former lives.

You would be stumped, wouldn't you, if someone were to ask you how to create a particular convolution of the brain so that its windings correspond to what they acquired in their previous life? If asked whether such a convolution should tend this way or that, you would not be able to decide. With the consciousness you have on the physical plane you could not say how to create brain convolutions corresponding, say, to the fact that a person was a good speaker in a previous life, how to elaborate the brain accordingly. Between death and rebirth, though, a person has to find an answer to this, must lay down in the new etheric body this finely, intricately sculpted structure of their organs. All this must be done. What is necessary for this to be done can easily be summed up in a single word, but I first wanted to invoke a feeling of the scope of this one word: wisdom is necessary, wisdom! And this wisdom must really be present in us. [...]

But it is different for those who die young: their etheric body has not 'juvenated' so much yet, and this means that there is less wisdom stored up in this etheric body acquired on earth—for it is really a matter of wisdom acquired on earth. Instead it contains something else: in the old, not yet 'juvenated' etheric body of someone who dies young, all the more will is present, a direct element of will, of love, a creative element of love. This, you see, is the difference between the etheric body of someone who has grown old, which is more imbued with the character of wisdom, and the etheric body of a person who dies young, which is imbued with the element of will. The etheric body of a person who has died young radiates love, warm love, warm, etheric love.

The etheric body of an old person radiates an aura of wisdom, of light.

Now we can answer the question of interest here by asking spiritual science what would happen if all people were to grow to be 80 or 90 years old, and if no one died young. In this case all the etheric bodies from which souls departed would be pervaded by loving wisdom. In their historical trajectory, human beings on earth would be able to learn a great deal on the earth between birth and death, for their physical bodies would be fashioned with great wisdom. In a sense, people would be born undifferentiated, they would resemble each other much more closely, but would be able to learn a great deal on the physical plane. We can say that they would be formed and structured with subtle wisdom, and could learn a great deal here on the physical plane. Yet such learning would be associated with an extremely unstable constitution. Because their physical organization would be so extremely finely configured with what I will call a 'mechanistic wisdom', they would have a fragile and easily lost equilibrium. A person would be able to learn a very great deal but would become terribly nervous, as we say today in our 'nervous epoch'. A very fidgety humanity would come into being, people would keep losing their equilibrium: a humanity very gifted in learning things on the physical plane but very twitchy at the same time. It's thought better to be called 'twitchy' than 'nervous'. [...] But if all human beings grew to be old and no one died young, there would not be the differentiation of soul we bring with us when we enter incarnation from the world of spirit. There would be a complete lack of predisposition, of being equipped with spiritual gifts. People would all enter life as fairly identical beings, undifferentiated, and would only become different by virtue of entering into different conditions on the physical plane, learning different things therefore. But they would cope with all circumstances in a fairly identical way. Karma would lead them through inherited physical traits into what was particularly apt for them, but otherwise there would be lacking in the world what we possess as specific inner pre-dispositions and potential. There would not be inner differ-entiation between people as we know it.

Yet in the same way that everything in the world must depend not on one-sidedness, as I have explained, but on balance, so human life must depend, firstly, on a person being able to pour into their physical organism what accu-mulates as wisdom for a subsequent physical life through the juvenescence of the etheric body. [And secondly, the will impulses of those who die young are needed.] I have offered many examples of how children who die young leave their etheric body unused. We ourselves, in this building, live in the aura of an etheric body, as I described. From this etheric body come the impulses that can inspire the artistic impulses at work in this building. I have told you how a child who belongs to this building left behind his etheric body after death, and this etheric body creates an aura in which this building is embedded. And if we can perceive the nature of the impulses that come from this etheric body, we gain support for the artistic impulses that must come to expres-sion in this building.

But this is how it is altogether with the etheric bodies of those who die young; they return, and have not yet grown so young again as to have completely weakened the element of the will, but rather will, the creative power of love, returns with them to the world of spirit. And now a continual interplay has to occur between the very 'juvenated' etheric bodies and those that are less so. Mutual support and reciprocity occurs continually in the spiritual world between etheric bodies rising from the earth from very old people, and the etheric bodies of young people, or of course of those neither young nor old. When very young children die—called in Goethe's *Faust,* the 'midnight-born'—their etheric bodies are very old, senescent, yet strong in will. Such etheric bodies will be able to work vigorously upon those that have passed through a long life, that come from the old.

Think how brilliant it was of Goethe to surround the 100-year-old Faust when he ascends to heaven with the etheric bodies of very young boys, the 'midnight-born', hinting at the interplay that must necessarily take place.

This mutual interplay continually occurs. And so we can say that in the world of spirit we have the etheric bodies of people who have grown physically old, and in whom various things occur; and then the etheric bodies of those who have died physically young, in whom various things likewise occur: and then a reciprocal exchange takes place, and what we encounter in the life between death and rebirth is found by virtue of the fact that realities are called forth through this exchange between the etheric bodies of those who have died young and those who have died when old. We need this mutual exchange. Humanity's evolution on earth could never develop in the right way if this reciprocal effect did not occur in the spirit world between the etheric bodies of young departed souls and those of people who die when old.

Those governing this activity are found in the region of the hierarchy of the angeloi, so that we really have to acknowledge this interaction between one kind of etheric body and another in the spiritual world in which we are embedded. Like two rivers flowing together and joining, a confluence of these influences occurs. But then they are ordered, regulated, governed in the right way. And this is done by beings from the hierarchy of the angeloi. Alongside other tasks they also have this one. Thus if a person with special potential is born, this is possible because, beside the means to inform physical bodies between death and rebirth with wisdom of a materialistic kind, wisdom gathered on earth, there are also influences present from what never fully developed on earth, coming from the etheric bodies of those who have died young, as forces that can be interwoven also when human potentialities and predispositions are created.

So you see how spiritual science, if we really enter into its secrets, can culminate in living feeling and sensibility. When an old person dies, the science of the spirit can enable us to raise our gaze to the spiritual mystery of their death. And this is because we know that people grow old so that humanity's evolution can progress in the right way in all future times, in that human beings will properly employ their bodily instruments. In every death of an old person we can intimate, feel in advance, the fruits of humanity's future evolution. And then we can let the opposite affect us, so that we gain the insight, as we look toward the future, that in humanity's further evolution there must always also be particular gifts and predispositions in people: one person must have a gift for one thing, another person a gift for another. People must bring diverse potential with them, even to the point of genius. And this could never be so if people did not also die young. If we look at particularly brilliant individuals, geniuses, they owe their genius to the fact that people also die young. So even the death of young people, the mystery of their death, is wisely interwoven with the whole of our evolutionary fabric, for these early deaths provide the seeds for soul capacities that humanity needs in its further evolution.

As soon as we can raise ourselves from our personal feelings about death to what the whole of humanity needs, we can glimpse the wisdom at work in the death of both young and old people. This is the significant thing: that spiritual science, if pursued with truth and authenticity, does not give us mere theories, but that the theories, if rightly understood, always culminate in feeling apprehensions that can give us greater harmony in life than we would otherwise have. We need the deeper reach and gaze of spiritual science so that, beyond the inevitable dissonances we experience in life, which sometimes seem unendurable, we can find our way through to the harmony underlying them.

Through spiritual science, too, we learn to understand the sacrifices we have to make in life. We come to understand many things that cause us pain if we know that the whole universe can only survive in its right and proper wisdom because of the pain we have to feel. Without the ground prepared by the death of young people, if we can only raise ourselves to sense and feel this, we would not have had the geniuses on whom humanity's evolution depends, such as Homer, Shakespeare, Goethe, Michelangelo, Raphael, and hundreds and hundreds more.

This has nothing to do with the particular individuality of those who die young: they sacrifice their etheric body in youth to the whole cosmos as a fertile soil upon which inner capacities and predispositions of soul can grow and ripen for humankind.

We grow together with the universe when we do not absorb spiritual science in the abstract but through it seek impulses that flow warmly into our souls, that reconcile us with the world, that deeply engage our soul, showing us that though we must endure pain, this is for the sake of the harmony of the whole universe.

It is not always easy to divert our gaze in this way from an individual human life to the life of the whole world. But the very difficulty of the enterprise strengthens our powers. By acquiring, through pain, a feeling for the whole, this sense of the whole world order will take deeper and more intimate root within our soul. And by this means we will prepare ourselves to become part of the world order in a way that is useful to the gods.[74]

> In a lecture given on 20 February 1913, Steiner describes how lofty angelic beings are dependent, in fulfilling their heavenly tasks, on collaboration with the souls of those who die young. Souls with a deeply materialistic inclination are in danger of lapsing from cosmic evolution, and this puts their reincarnation at risk. Even beings of the higher hierarchies can only alter this by drawing on an additional influx of powers in the form of unused etheric substance from those who die young.

But let us continue by asking this: what happens with the souls whose destiny it is here on earth to die in the flower of youth, to be carried off by plagues and suchlike? What happens with these souls when they pass through the portal of death prematurely and enter the world of spirit?

We can discover the destiny of these souls if, with clairvoyant vision, we delve as it were into the activity of spirits who accompany and help govern the evolution of the earth, or evolution in general. These beings of the higher hierarchies have certain forces, certain powers to advance evolution. Yet there is a certain limit to these powers and potencies. The following is true, for instance: in our own era very materialistic souls, who lose all sense of the world of spirit, are in danger of demise, of being cut off in some ways from the ongoing course of evolution. In our times already a large part of humanity is at risk of being left behind, of being kept back on earth through their own soul weight because they are highly materialistic, and so failing to move onward to their next incarnation. But the higher hierarchies have resolved to avert this danger. In truth, the decisive hour for souls who have cut themselves off from evolution and cannot continue in its stream will only arrive in the sixth epoch, and ultimately only during the early stages of Venus evolution. Souls are not yet to fall into weight to such a degree that they must remain stranded. The higher hierarchies have resolved to prevent this. But these beings of the higher hierarchies are to some degree limited in their powers and capacities. Nothing enjoys unlimited powers, not even amongst the higher angelic hierarchies. And if everything depended only on their powers, very materialistic souls would already inevitably, by their own nature, become cut off in a certain way from the stream of ongoing evolution. By their own powers these beings of the higher hierarchies cannot really save such souls, but they can draw on a remedy. The souls of those who die young, you see, still have unused potential. Let us say they die in some catastrophe—run over by an express train for instance. Such a soul gives up its sheath and is now free of the body, deprived of the body, and yet it still possesses all the powers that would otherwise be able to act and work in the body on earth. When such souls rise into the world of spirit they bring with them very particular powers that could actually still act here on earth, but are prematurely diverted from doing so. Such forces are of special use, and are indeed used by the beings of the higher hierarchies to save the souls who cannot save themselves by their own powers.

Souls with a materialistic outlook are thus conducted onward into better times and saved, since their powers are equipped only for the regular course of humanity's evolution. They are saved because the higher hierarchies gain an access of strength in the form of unused powers, rising to them from the earth, which still retain an unused energy dynamic. These forces accrue to the beings of the higher hierarchies. And therefore souls who die prematurely help their fellow human beings who would otherwise sink deep into the mire of materialism.[75]

> Three weeks after Rudolf Steiner had spoken of this continuing influence of the forces of those who die prematurely, he spoke again, in Munich, about the collaboration of human souls with lofty angelic beings. He again emphasized how 'significant' these souls are for the spiritual world, and spoke of their powers being employed 'in the loveliest way'.

But there is a further means of creating compensatory balance, present in a different way; and this shows us how even the grim and gloomy aspects of human existence are also embedded in the world's universal wisdom. Even when we encounter something that must initially burden and depress us, we can raise our spirits again by considering what may be called its equivalent in the whole fabric of existence. If, for instance, we think of people who depart this life in the flower of their youth through accident or illness, we can see how such souls laid aside their physical body before it had been depleted and exhausted, how the sheath of which they are divested would otherwise have served, if they had lived, to shape existence in their physical body. They bear these forces with them as they rise to a higher world of spirit at death. Such souls enter supersensible worlds in a way different from those who have lived the full term of their life on earth.

It is highly significant to observe such souls after they have passed through the portal of death, souls who have died in the flower of their youth, losing their corporeal sheath through an accident, and to trace their further existence. They bear upward into higher worlds powers which would otherwise have served their physical life on earth. What happens with these powers?

They are used in the supersensible world in the loveliest way. If we study the beings of the higher hierarchies who govern and guide the ongoing course of evolution, we find them to be endowed with the forces essential to this evolution. Yet—and this is not an imperfection in the world, but relates to other perfections—all powers, even those of the higher hierarchies, are to some degree limited, are not infinite. These spirits support all advancement including progress between death and a new birth, but there are many earthly human beings who, arriving as souls in the world of spirit after they die, have a nature that is beyond the power of the spirits of the higher hierarchies to deal with. I have often stated, and it is true, that we do not as yet need to despair about souls who are thoroughly materialistic, who close themselves off from the world of spirit, and do not wish to understand the ideas we need today about the supersensible world. But when such souls arrive in the spiritual world after death, it is in some respects difficult for the spiritual beings of the higher hierarchies to do anything much with them. You see, these beings of the higher hierarchies have the powers needed for the progressive course of humanity's evolution, but only for this *progressive* development. If souls close themselves completely to this progressive evolution, then they have, in a sense, a weight too great for the spirits of the higher hierarchies to overcome. As I have said, it is true that we do not yet need to despair about the fate of these souls, since this will only become dangerous for them in the sixth post-Atlantean epoch; and only in the Venus era could they be discarded entirely from the onward course of evolution. But if the beings of the higher hierarchies who support progressive evolution had nothing but the powers with which they are equipped, then they would not be able to do anything with these souls and they would lapse far sooner from the ongoing course of evolution.[76]

> Losing someone can trigger deep grief in the those left behind, whether the deceased was young or old. But the spiritual observer finds great differences in perspective from souls who died at different ages. Children often remain closely connected with us; they do not wish to leave, and therefore transfer their pain to their living relatives. The pain felt by the bereft family is one of sympathy. Those who die in old age, on the other hand, do not feel such a stark separation, and maintain connections in their own way. The pain of the grieving in this case is more egoistic in nature.

It makes a great difference whether young children who have loved us die, or whether older people die leaving us younger ones behind. The following can characterize this difference in a way that accords with experience in the world of spirit. When young children die, the secret of our community with them can be expressed by saying we do not actually lose them, spiritually speaking. They remain present spiritually. Children who die young are always spiritually very present.

We will look at this more closely in a moment. But first let me offer you, as a meditation for further reflection, the thought that children are not lost to us when they die, but always remain spiritually present. The opposite is true of older people who die: we can say that *they* do not lose us. We do not lose children when they die, and older people do not lose us when they die. When old people die they feel a strong pull toward the world of spirit, but this also gives them the power to engage with the physical world so as to approach us more easily. While they go further off from the physical world than children, who stay close to us, they are furnished with greater powers of perception than those who die at a younger age. They retain us. As one becomes acquainted with diverse souls in the world of spirit, whether they died when they were young or old, one discovers that those who died at a later age have the power more easily to enter into earthly souls, and not to lose them, while children remain more or less within the sphere of earthly human beings, and so we do not lose them. [. . .]

In respect of the pain people feel at the loss of someone, they do not generally discriminate between the death of a young or old person. And yet, seen spiritually, there is a very great difference between the two. We can say that someone who loses a child, whether their own or one they have loved, feels—to use something of a 'technical' term—a certain 'sympathetic pain'. Children stay with us, really, and because we were connected with them and they remain so close to us, they transfer their pain to our souls, so that we feel their pain at desiring still to be here. Because we share their pain, it is easier for them to bear. Dead children really feel within us. It is good if we can feel with them, for this eases their pain. By contrast, the pain we feel when older people die, whether parents or friends, can be called an egoistic pain. A person who dies when older does not lose us. Here in our body we have the sense that we have lost them, and so the pain we feel only concerns ourselves. It is an egoistic pain. We are not feeling the dead person's pain as we do with children, but just our own, for ourselves.

We can actually distinguish these two types of pain very precisely: egoistic pain at the death of older people, sympathetic pain for younger ones. The child goes on living within us. We are sad only in ourselves really at the death of older people. This is not insignificant.[77]

> Some lives on earth end before they have properly begun. Meaning can be found even in that. This may be a way in which the imperfection of a past life rounds out to wholeness.

What does it mean for a child to be born, live only a few days, then die? Esoteric science can teach us that a life as brief as this nevertheless has meaning. The being in this child's body may often have been able to develop many things but was perhaps deficient in a particular respect—in healthy vision, for instance. Let's assume that in one incarnation a person was an excellent human being but had a visual weakness. In this case, the soul may later live for only a few days in a following incarnation, simply to redress what they lacked in their past life because of their weak eyes. Should this happen, we would count this brief incarnation as part of the previous life. People generally greatly underestimate the child's learning capacity in the first few days of life. The child needs greater capacity when learning to look at light than a university student needs to learn everything in their first academic term.[78]

Karmic laws

Rudolf Steiner saw it as one of his most important missions to embed the laws of reincarnation and karma in Christian culture. Karmic laws reveal the causes and effects of our actions from one life to another. They do not conflict with our human potential for freedom, but can, rather, be regarded in terms of opportunities and tasks—as well as challenges and hindrances—that aid us in growing ever more human. Steiner presented his karma research in numerous texts and lectures. We can cite here only a few aspects, directly relating to our experiences in old age. First comes a passage in which Steiner explains the way in which karma works in general.

Let us consider how karma specifically works. If we look at a person's actions, we can always discover a *disposition of character* underlying them. One and the same action can be instigated by a variety of different motives. The action and its consequences will initially lead to a favourable or unfavourable outcome in our present life. A person's character, inclinations and habits also inform their karma: these qualities remain configured in the etheric body and in a following life are assimilated into the physical body. They transform themselves into organ-configuring forces in the physical body in the person's subsequent life. And since the properties of our etheric body influence our physical body in a following life, our weak or healthy organization in this life depends upon our inclinations and habits in the previous one. Thus we can affect the nature of our next life by cultivating noble inclinations and feelings in our present incarnation, in this way ensuring that our body will be strong and sound in our next incarnation. The causes of illness are in fact moral. [. . .]

Since the moral qualities we cultivate have a corporeal effect in future generations, living morally means that we live not only for ourselves but also nurture the health of future generations.[79]

> In a lecture in 1912, in Vienna, Rudolf Steiner elaborated on possible karmic connections in family relationships with parents, siblings or other close relatives. Often these people belong to a group with whom, in a previous life, we shared common experiences at around the age of 30. Steiner encourages us to provisionally conceive of such destiny relationships, though we should avoid pursuing such ideas to flatter our desires or prejudices. In this context he also speaks of the encounters we have in the second half of life. Here, in particular, redress often occurs for incisive events in a previous life with people to whom our karma leads us again. Thus 'threads of karma spun' in one life find their conclusion and resolution in the next.

On the other hand, we discover something very remarkable. The people we encountered in our earliest infancy—parents, siblings, playmates or others in our surroundings then—are usually those who were our friends or acquaintances at around the age of 30 in a previous incarnation. It often turns out that such people become our parents or siblings in the present incarnation. Although this may sound somewhat curious, you can try applying it to your own life, and you will find that life does become more brightly illumined from this perspective. If it is not so, simply testing it provisionally will do no harm. It is hugely beneficial for us to take quiet, secluded moments of reflection when we observe life in a way that gives it meaning. We must just make sure we do not follow our predilections when doing so—not trying to arrange things so that we imagine our parents will be the people we would particularly like to have. Preconception can easily shed a false light on things. A danger lies in wait here, along with countless preconceptions. Yet such reflections are valuable if we cultivate freedom from preconception in these complex matters.

But you may ask about the second half of life too. The people around us in infancy in this life we find, remarkably, to be ones with whom we were acquainted in the middle of our former life. But what about the second half of life? In our declining years, we are brought together with people with whom we may have had a connection in a past life, but may also not have done. We can tell that they had something to do with us in our past life if special, characteristic things occur, as they so often do at some decisive point—let us say, a severe trial involving bitter disappointment. In the second half of life, in relation to such occurrences, we are brought together with people who were in one way or another connected with us previously. Through the shift in circumstances thus caused, many things originating in a former life are redressed.

This makes things diverse and complex, and shows us we cannot regard them too schematically. In the second half of life, especially, we encounter people with whom the threads of karma spun in one life could be finally dealt with in the next. Let us imagine we did someone a wrong in one life. It would be easy to assume that in a following life we are brought together with this person again, and that the wiser one within us will arrange this so that we can make recompense for what we did to them. But the circumstances of life are not always such that we can rebalance everything—often only partial redress is possible. This makes necessary things that complicate matters, and which mean that such residues of previous karma can at last be balanced out in the second half of [a further] life.[80]

> In 1924, Rudolf Steiner gave over 80 'karma lectures' as they were called. In the lecture of 1 March, he spoke among other things of karmic connections in friendships. A breakdown in a friendship of our youth can be caused by an overly egoistic friendship in older years in a past life.

Now something else must occur in life if this impulse, to be close to someone in youth, does not nevertheless mature into remaining friends when we are older. In all the cases I am aware of, I always found that if these people remained united in a later life, if this friendship of their youth did not rupture, they would subsequently weary of each other because in a former life they had developed the friendship—one formed in later years—too egoistically. The egoism of friendships in one life is karmically avenged in further lives. That is how complex things are. But you can find a rule of thumb if you see that, in one life, it is often the case that two people lead separate lives until around the age of 20, and then form a friendship. In a next life on earth, this picture usually corresponds to another, that of a friendship in youth, after which they go their separate ways. That happens very frequently, and in general it is true to say that consecutive lives complement each other's configuration.

These things are a rule of thumb, not valid in every case, but one thing you find frequently is this: if you meet a person in the middle years of one incarnation who has a strong influence on your destiny, then it may well be that they had a close connection with you at the beginning and end of your life in a previous incarnation. Then we have this picture: in one incarnation you are close to the person at the beginning and end of your life, and in another incarnation you meet them, instead, in the middle of life, and not at the beginning and end.

Or it may be that we have a close connection of destiny with someone in our childhood. In a past life, we were connected with this same person shortly before we died. Such mirrorings occur very frequently indeed in destiny connections.[81]

> Karmic laws are tangible and specific. Every night, already, we carry into the spirit world what is to take effect in future. In collaboration with the beings of higher hierarchies a foundation is laid here for the way in which our future earthly body can be 'woven' after death. Human love and hate lead to physical effects in our next life. The soul force of one life acts upon the corporeal nature of the next.

If we think in materialistic terms, we will say that people are resting when they sleep. But they are not only resting. If we develop the right kind of idealism during waking life, we carry into sleep a capacity enabling the astral body to raise itself aloft to the hierarchy of the angeloi, or in other words to enter in sleep into the kind of relationship with the world of spirit that will allow us to live rightly through the time from death to a new birth. Of course, if we do not live rightly through this period, we also bear frailties back with us into earthly life. How we succeed in fashioning our next life depends on the way in which we develop the right relationship to the primordial powers, to the archai. We find, therefore, that universal human love has a creative power. For what does it depend on if someone is strong and energetic in one life, and able to place their physical body at the service of their soul, to master their physical body? It depends on whether they developed love of humanity, a purely inner soul quality, in their previous incarnation.

You will recall me saying in earlier lectures that the soul nature of one life on earth comes to expression in the physical nature of a subsequent incarnation, and the spiritual quality of one life manifests in the soul nature of a next one. But things are as I just described them.

You cannot assert that there is something like destiny, karma, in general terms, but only that one can perceive how a person is working on their karma. We weave it while asleep, and when we are awake harvest what we need for the weaving. What we weave are the threads we must spin from universal human love; or threads that continually rupture and create bad karma for our next life—those woven of hatred of human beings. The creative forces at work in karma are, above all, those of love or hatred of humankind.[82]

> Karmic connections can also however emerge within a single life on earth, as Rudolf Steiner showed on 22 December 1909. In this lecture he described the subtle consequences of a noble anger erupting in youth. Such anger—perhaps in idealistic outrage against injustice—can reappear transformed in later years as loving kindness and the power to bless.

This noble anger of youth pervades the soul and gradually transforms during the course of life. In doing so, it re-emerges in the second half of life in a different form: as a mood of loving gentleness and the capacity to bless. In other words, the noble anger of youth in earlier life resurfaces in later life as loving kindness, as a blessed disposition. And it will be unlikely—all things being equal—to find this loving kindness, this ability to bless in later years if it has not first manifested in youth as noble anger, in response to stupidity or ugliness. Thus we find a karmic connection in ordinary life, which we could clothe in an image by saying this: A hand that was not able to clench in noble anger in youth will not reach out to bless in our later years.[83]

> 'To die before the age of 35 is not to die in vain', said Rudolf Steiner on 18 November 1915. He describes this period of life as a 'bridge', after crossing which we establish a new and different connection with life. Those who die young retain unused forces that strengthen their future will. In the following life such a person can display an impetuous temperament. Those who do not die until after this 'crossing' will tend to be thoughtful and reflective in their next life, acquainting themselves more inwardly and intimately with the world, and ready perhaps to take up tasks that are not confined within the narrower bounds of their own contentment.

In brief, people are very different from each other in the way they act in life, and this, after all, makes life possible. For instance, there are people who do not care greatly about doing much in the way of outer deeds, and yet they only need let fall a word or a phrase and this affects people around them. Their influence proceeds more from their inward life, while others act more externally. This is intimately connected with how we have spent our life in a previous incarnation. Some die young, say before the age of 35, to take this as a kind of defining boundary. And this early death leaves them in a quite different position from those who die after that point. If you die before you are 35, you remain closer to the world from which you emerged at birth. And the age of 34 is an important boundary point, at which we cross a bridge in a sense, when the world we were born out of recedes, and instead we give birth more inwardly to a new world of spirit. It is important to distinguish this. Now when someone dies before the age of 35, and subsequently is reincarnated, the energy they did not expend in the period after 35 accrues to them in a way. In such people, who die before the age of 35, thus saving the forces they would otherwise have expended had they grown to be 50, 60 or 70, this surplus strength they have saved supplements the forces they incorporate into themselves when entering upon their next incarnation. This means that such souls are born in bodies that enable them, usually in their youth, to receive vivid, vigorous impressions.

In other words, if such souls died in their previous incarnation before the age of 35, when they reincarnate everything makes a strong impression on them. This can kindle anger in them; they can feel great pleasure, have lively feelings, and feel urged to rapid action. Such people gain a strong purchase on life, find their mission. To die before the age of 35 is not to die in vain, for this places us into life in a very particular way. But if we die after 35—though things are not always so straightforward, and dying before 35 can bring something different too, these are only examples, not to be taken as a hard and fast rule—this may mean that in our next life our surroundings do not make such a strong impression on us. We may be slower to feel enthusiasm or anger. We acquaint ourselves more slowly, and yet more intimately, with things, and because of this will grow into a subsequent incarnation in which we act more through inwardness, without being led so definitely to a life's mission. It may be then that we pursue a task in life that is not quite the one we might have wished for, but that can nevertheless be used to accomplish something special, perhaps even against our own will. Since our previous incarnation rendered us fit to act in subtler ways, we can serve tasks of broader scope.[84]

Lucifer and Ahriman

Youth and age are characterized by contrary principles, behind which stand active powers in the world of spirit. If these work in one-sided ways, youth and age can appear in caricature form. Youthful qualities manifest in spontaneity and mobility, and have a more feeling nature. Age, on the other hand, can grow into cautious deliberation or even harden into rigid immobility. Lucifer has an affinity with the first, with warmth, liveliness and—sometimes even fanatic—illusion. Ahriman's element, meanwhile, is calculating reason and the quest for outward power.

At the beginning of 1922, in a lecture considering the actions and effects of Lucifer and Ahriman within our being of body, soul and spirit, Rudolf Steiner described how both must act equally at every phase of life. In terms of illness, for instance, we find Lucifer at work in febrile and inflammatory conditions, and Ahriman in mineralizing and hardening ones. Health is found in the balance between such states.

Let us first reflect on something that starts with our corporeal nature. Our physical being is a unified entity only to outward, sense perception. In fact, we are continually harnessed between powers that, respectively, rejuvenate us and make us old, powers of birth and powers of death. At no single moment of life is only one of these powers present in our body. They are both always there.

In childhood, or infancy if you like, the rejuvenating, luciferic forces predominate, and yet, deeply withdrawn and bedded in human nature already, debilitating forces of age are also present, the forces that ultimately cause the body to calcify and become sclerotic, and eventually lead to death. Both types of forces are necessary in the human body. The luciferic forces within us continually enable us to develop, one can say, toward the phosphor pole, toward warmth. In an extreme instance, in illness, these forces engender fever, pleuritis, inflammatory conditions. But this tendency to fever, to inflammation, is always present in us: it is just kept in check, in balance, by the opposing forces that seek to solidify, calcify and mineralize us. And human nature consists in maintaining a balance between these two opposing dynamics.[85]

> Through the polar opposite actions of luciferic and ahrimanic powers, a field of tension develops between dissolution and consolidation. In his lecture of 29 January 1921, Steiner spoke of the deeper intentions of these two adversaries: Lucifer seeks to hinder maturation processes in earthly life by keeping people in the condition of childhood. Ahriman on the other hand wants to solidify us to such a degree that we remain chained to the earth, thus rupturing the alternation between earthly and spiritual existence.

The luciferic powers can hold us back in childhood in a sense, can prevent us from maturing. People who give themselves up too much to fantasy or fancifulness, to a nebulous mysticism, who are disinclined to engage in taut, well-configured thinking, who don't like clear ideas about the world; and those too who scorn inner soul work, the effort of developing keen inner responsiveness—thus people who more or less dream their way through life—will be at risk of being unable to grow old properly in their next incarnation, will remain childish in the negative sense. In this way a luciferic influx will make itself felt amongst humanity, and this would mean that people in their next incarnation would not fully immerse themselves in earthly life. You could say that they would not depart far enough from the world of spirit to enter into earthly life. The luciferic powers that once united with our earth endeavour to kindle instincts in us that will lead to humanity arriving at a stage of evolution when people remain like children, and do not properly age. The luciferic powers want to bring things to a point when there are no old people on earth, but instead people spend their lives in a kind of youthful fantasy. By this means the luciferic powers would make the earth a place, increasingly, that possesses one body as a whole planet, and one common soul in which the separate souls are merged. Lucifer is endeavouring to lead human evolution toward the earth having one soul nature and one bodily nature in common, to make as it were one whole organic being of the earth, with a common soul in which the separate souls lose their individuality. [...]

Ahrimanic beings, too, have united with our earth, and have the opposite tendency, acting above all through the forces that between birth and death draw our organism toward them, as it were, that entirely pervade our organism with mentality or in other words make us ever more intellectual, imbue us ever more with intellect. You see, our wakeful intelligence depends upon the soul's connection with the physical body, and when this connection grows excessive, we develop too much of an affinity with physical existence and lose equilibrium. And then a tendency appears that will prevent people in future from having the right alternation between life on earth and life in the spirit between death and a new birth.

It is Ahriman's endeavour to prevent human beings in

coming times from passing rightly through earth life and super-earthly life.[86]

> It is very important for humanity's future evolution for us to become aware of how soul and body nature is connected with the influences of both Lucifer and Ahriman upon our life on earth. In a lecture in 1913, Rudolf Steiner described how most people only become well acquainted with the influences of Lucifer and Ahriman in after-death existence, when they encounter these powers 'from without'. In future it will become ever more important that people also recognize Lucifer and Ahriman during earthly life. When the reality of these adversaries is overlooked or denied, they are able to expand their power unhindered, to the grave detriment of humanity.

Between birth and death, therefore, in our relationship with progressive spiritual beings, we find that we stand in a sense between Lucifer and Ahriman. And for the whole of human evolution to unfold in the right way, this relationship must be sustained between death and rebirth also. The difference is only that what remains inward in us between birth and death becomes outward, external, between death and rebirth. From the moment our memory begins in infancy, the moment to which we can remember back later, Lucifer has lodged his claws in the human soul. This is within us—we know nothing of it unless we learn of it through spiritual science, and learn to feel it. After death it is different. At a certain point Lucifer appears there too, just as surely as he appeared inwardly during our lifetime, but now, in the life between death and rebirth, he appears outwardly. He stands there fully before us, stands beside us, and we journey onward with him! Before we pass through the portal of death we are unaware of Lucifer, but now we know and perceive him as he accompanies us between death and rebirth. In our present cycle of time, this can be a very unpleasant awareness. We can pass through the realm between death and rebirth in a sense accompanied by Lucifer, and having insight into his necessity to the world: he not only has a dreadful quality but also something beautiful, a glorious outward form. The time is increasingly approaching when people will only be able to pass through the life after death accompanied in this way by Lucifer if they have been able properly to acquaint themselves with Lucifer, to have an intimation of him, here in this life. Those who wish to know nothing about Lucifer while on earth—and as we move toward the future there will be ever more of these, no doubt the majority—will learn all the more of Lucifer after death. Not only will he stand beside them but he will tap or siphon off their soul forces, will vampirize them. This vampirization is what people are preparing for themselves by ignorance, and it means they will be losing forces for their next life, forces that they relinquish in a sense to Lucifer.

Something very similar is true in relation to Ahriman. Things are as follows in relation to him. Both these spirits are always present between death and a new birth, but sometimes one of them is more present and the other less, and then vice versa. In the life between death and rebirth we have an outward and then a return journey. On our outward passage, Lucifer accompanies us particularly, while on the return path toward birth, Ahriman, especially, is by our side. He leads us back to earth, is an important figure in our return journey in the second half of this period. And he too can inflict bad things on those who do not wish to believe in him in their life between birth and death: he gives them too many of his forces. He endows them with what he always has in excess, the forces connected with earthly gravity, that can introduce into earthly existence illness and premature death, all kinds of misfortunes that appear to be random, and so forth. All this is connected with these ahrimanic powers.[87]

> Ahriman acts within everything that is formed and shaped. We owe our physical resilience to him. But he can employ his capacities to deceive people. The appearance of a double is a phenomenon known both in psychopathology and literature. Steiner himself presented such a figure in dramatic form. In a talk in Munich on 30 August 1913, to accompany the performance of his mystery plays, he explained how experiences of the double come about. From unconscious soul aspects or fragments that have separated from the human being, Ahriman shapes a figure who suddenly and unexpectedly confronts the 'original'.

Within the human soul are parts that one can in a sense separate off from the soul's entirety. And because we do not exercise complete sway over such occlusions, Ahriman seizes on them. And through Ahriman's unjustified activity, which exceeds his due bounds, a tendency arises for these parts of our etheric and astral nature, which tend to separate from the rest of our soul life and become autonomous, to be formed and shaped by Ahriman into a human figure. Basically, all kinds of thoughts we harbour within us can assume human form. And when we encounter these thoughts as thought-beings, when Ahriman has the opportunity to autonomize a part of the human soul in this way, to give it a human form, then we can encounter this autonomous part of our being as a double when we enter the elemental world. It is always a part of the human soul to which Ahriman gives human form. We just have to recognize that, when entering the elemental world, when outside the body, circumstances alter a great deal. When we are inside our physical body we cannot confront ourselves in this way; but when we enter the elemental world in our etheric body, we can both be within it and yet see it from without, in the same way that we see the double. Basically, in terms of substance, the double is a major part of the etheric body itself. While we retain a part of it, a part separates off, becomes objective. We regard it: it is part of our own being, a part to which Ahriman has given the form that we ourselves have. You see, Ahriman tries to compress everything into the laws of the physical world. In the physical world the spirits of form hold sway, and they share this dominion with Ahriman—so that he can certainly do what we can describe as shaping a part of our human nature into the double.

This encounter with the double is—relatively speaking—an elemental phenomenon, and it can arise through particular subconscious impressions and impulses of the human soul even if a person is not clairvoyant. Something like the following can occur. A person can practise intrigue, can have inflicted evil on others through his intrigues. Let's imagine he goes out one day and engineers some kind of intrigue, then returns home, goes to his study where, on the desk, papers are lying on which are written things he has used to contrive his intrigues. Even though his conscious mind may be of a cynical bent, these impulses of intrigue may nevertheless seize hold of his subconscious. He goes into his study, looks at his desk—and sees himself sitting there. Such things are common, and can occur especially when some kind of intrigue is happening. What you encounter there is certainly the double I sought to portray, though with other aims, in *The Guardian of the Threshold* and *The Soul's Awakening*. It is

part of the singular development of Johannes Thomasius that
he has these encounters with the double, arising from his
distinctive experiences: Ahriman can shape a part of his soul
in such a way that this part is substantially filled with self-
seeking soul elements, as an aspect of the etheric body.[88]

The corpse as ferment

> Immediately after the founding of the Waldorf School in
> Stuttgart in September 1919, Rudolf Steiner returned to
> Dornach and took up a theme that he had been addressing
> with the teachers there. He spoke of the threefold human
> being, and of how we belong integrally to both the earth and
> the cosmos. In this context he spoke also of the importance
> that a human life and the physical corpse have beyond death.
> Through the human corpse, he said, soul-spiritual 'forces of
> renewal' enter the earth organism, supplying it with sub-
> stance and hindering the universal death process. The
> planet would long since have withered if human beings did
> not live and die upon it.

You see, what is given back to the earth, irrespective of
whether the body is cremated or buried, once had human
form and had this also by virtue of the fact that before
birth, or before conception, a being of spirit and soul descended from worlds of spirit and worked within this physical body until death. Then this physical body is given to
the earth; and the nature of human form works on in the
earth, irrespective of whether the body was cremated or
buried, and continues to collaborate with the earth. To the
earth is continually imparted something that it would not
have if human bodies were not given up to it at death; the
earth benefits from this. Otherwise, if it did not receive

human bodies, the earth would only possess earthly substances.

A being of soul and spirit lived in this human body, descending before birth or conception from worlds of soul and spirit, and configuring this human body. This configuration remains as something essential in every grain of dust, enters the earth or the atmosphere at cremation or burial, and with this human body the earth receives what descended from spiritual worlds. This is not without significance. It is not even an ordinary, everyday truth but has very great significance. You see our earth is no longer evolving, and it would have long been the case that no human being could dwell upon it, perhaps not animals either—or perhaps animals could—if it did not continually receive rejuvenating, soul-spiritual forces in the form of human bodies. The earth is still habitable for humankind because it continually receives human bodies which keep refreshing and rejuvenating it. Since the middle of Atlantean times, the earth intrinsically has already been withering, and no longer has forces of uplift any more, which it did possess in the ancient Polaric time and in Lemurian times and so forth. Since the middle of the Atlantean period, the earth as such only has forces of withering, and is refreshed and sustained only by receiving the formative powers of human bodies which work on in the earth. Only they make the earth a place still habitable for human beings.

You can see from this that on the one hand the inner forces of the planet are active within us, the forces of the atmosphere. But we also give back soul-spiritual forces to the earth; we supply the earth with soul-spiritual forces. When we are born we bear soul-spiritual forces from the spiritual universe into the earthly realm, and use them as long as we

need them, until death; then we give them to the earth as
formative powers and so become collaborators helping to
shape the future earth. [. . .]

Someone who knows themselves to be a citizen of the
cosmos realizes that by entering this existence at birth they
bear into this world a soul-spiritual element, and that at
death, when they depart this earth, they also continue to
contribute to the edifice of future earth existence. Only as a
citizen of the cosmos does a person recognize fully how their
existence is connected with earthly existence—how they are
one being with it, and by being so basically endow the earth
with its spirituality.[89]

> In his introductory pedagogical course in Stuttgart, Rudolf
> Steiner had previously conjured this vivid picture of the
> corpse as a kind of ferment that sustains the earth's further
> evolution. In the course of life, forces accumulate in the
> human body and are transformed, and at death, given up to
> the earth, can continue to act with fertilizing effect.

In the same way, though, earthly evolution would long since
have reached its end stage if the forces of the human corpse,
sundered at death from the spirit and soul, were not given up
to it. These forces, which continually accrue to earthly evolution from human corpses, sustain it. Minerals, that would
otherwise have long ceased to develop their crystallization
forces, can go on doing so in consequence. They would
otherwise have long since crumbled and dissolved. And this
means also that plants, that would long since have ceased to
grow, can continue to do so. The same is true of the lower
animal forms. With our corpse we give the earth a ferment, a
kind of yeast for further evolution.

Whether or not human beings live on the earth is therefore

not meaningless. It simply is not true that the earth with its mineral, plant and animal kingdoms would continue to evolve if the human being did not exist. The process at work in nature is a unified whole to which the human being belongs. We only rightly conceive of human beings if we think of them as participating in the whole cosmic process, even furthering it with their death.

If you consider this you will scarcely be surprised if I also say the following. When we descend from the world of spirit into the physical world, we receive the garment of our physical body. But naturally the physical body is different when we receive it as a child from when we discard it at death, at whatever age. Something has happened with it; and what has happened can only happen by virtue of the fact that this body has been infused with the human being's forces of soul and spirit. Ultimately of course we eat the same things that animals eat, that is, we transform and assimilate outer substances just as animals do, but we do so with the participation of something that animals do not possess, something that descends from the world of spirit and unites with the human being's physical body. In consequence, we make of these substances something other than animals and plants make of them. And the substances that are given up to the earth in the human corpse are transformed ones, are different in nature from what we received when we were born. And so we can say that during our lifetime we renew the substances we receive and the forces, too, which we receive at birth, and then give them back transformed to the earth process. The substances and forces we give up to the earth process at death are not the same as those we received at birth. Thus we give to the physical-sensory earth process something that continually flows into it through us from the supersensible world.

At birth we bear something with us down from the super-sensible world; and the earth receives this when we die by virtue of the fact that we incorporate it into the substances and forces that constitute our body during our lifetime. By this means we continually infuse physical, sensory reality with something supersensible: this trickles or rains down if you like from the supersensible to the physical realm, but these falling drops would remain unfruitful for the earth if we human beings did not absorb them and, through ourselves, mediate them to the earth. We absorb these drops at birth and give them up at death, and they continually fertilize the earth with supersensible forces, and sustain the earth's evolutionary process. Without human corpses, therefore, the earth would long since have died.[90]

Living with the dead

'Every one of us continually consorts with the so-called dead,' said Rudolf Steiner on 14 February 1918. However, this is mostly an unconscious process, and, to be consciously cultivated, requires special attentiveness at moments when we fall asleep and awaken. If we vividly call a dead person to mind, the contact with them is easier to sustain.

We do consort with the dead, and this contact is especially present at the moments when we fall asleep and reawaken. In fact, at the moment of falling asleep, every person asks countless questions and sends countless messages to beloved dead souls. But it is possible to cultivate this communication in a certain way. We have often talked of some of the ways in which this can be done, but today the following will be said. [...]

As long as we do not live in a purely egoistic and sensory way, we will have a sound instinct about the need for communication to continue with certain individuals with whom karma has connected us, who have crossed the threshold of death either recently or longer ago. Assuredly we will often send our thoughts to people who have died. It can certainly be the case that such thoughts, which invoke for us a memory of dead people, give rise to real communication with these dead, even if we are unaware of this, and even if we are unable to attend to what happens at the moments when we fall asleep. But some thoughts are more favourable for such communication and others less favourable. Abstract thoughts, ones we harbour with some indifference, or perhaps even out of a sense of duty, will not easily find their way to a dead soul as we fall asleep. On the other hand, thoughts and pictures that arise from a sense of special interest that united us with these dead when they were alive, will find their way to them. If we recall the dead person not just with cool, abstract thoughts but instead recall a moment when we grew warm in their presence, when something they said was of some moment, was something loving—moments we spent with the person in a commonality of feeling, of shared will impulses also, when we undertook something with them or resolved upon something together that we both valued and led us to a shared endeavour, or in brief something that let our hearts resonate together harmoniously—then, if we bring this harmony of our hearts vividly to mind, it colours our thoughts of the dead, which take wing toward them the next time we fall asleep. Whatever time of day we do this—nine in the morning, midday, two o'clock—any point in the whole day can give us a moment to harbour such a thought, and it will remain in us and pass to the dead at the moment we fall asleep.

At the moment we wake again, we can receive an answer, a message, communications from the dead. If we are unable to attend to this moment it does not necessarily matter for the response can, as we believe if we believe in such things at all, emerge from our soul somehow during the course of the day in the form of a sudden insight or thought. But here again there is a more favourable and less favourable way of cultivating this. Under certain circumstances, the dead more easily find access to us, to utter this or that into our soul so that it speaks from within our soul itself. In other circumstances it is less easy. Most favourable are circumstances in which we have formed a good, accurate picture of the nature of the dead person, having such keen interest in their being that they stand in vivid reality before our eye of spirit. You will ask why I say this. If you have been close to someone, you will think, you surely have a clear picture of their being. But I don't believe so, especially not in our times. In our times people pass each other by like ships in the night, know each other very little. This may not particularly distance us from each other here in the physical world but it does estrange us from each other a very great deal for the world through which the dead pass. You see, for here, for the physical world, there are numerous unconscious or subconscious forces and impulses that bring people close to one another, even if they do not wish to really know each other. As some of you may have read, you can be married to a person for decades and still actually know each other very little. And then there are other impulses that bring people together and do not depend on mutual knowledge. Life is filled with subconscious and unconscious impulses. But, as we said, these subconscious impulses connect us here, bind us to each other, but do not bind us with those who have passed on before us through death. To remain connected we really have to absorb into our soul something that allows the being of the other to live vividly within us. And the more alive they become within us, the easier they gain access to our soul and the more easily they can communicate with us.

That is what I wished to describe in relation to our continuing, always and ever-recurring dialogue between the so-called living and the so-called dead. Each of us continually consorts with the so-called dead, and people only do not know of this because they are unable to sufficiently observe the moment of falling asleep, the moment of awakening. I say this to give you a clearer and more tangible sense of our coexistence with the supersensible world in which the dead live.[91]

> Our relationship with the dead during sleep is of great importance for both realms. The souls of the dead actively seek this contact with us, as Rudolf Steiner describes in a lecture on 10 October 1913.

Just as we on earth—if I may use this metaphor—must have our fields to cultivate crops, which nourish us and give us physical life on earth, so the souls of the dead must have their fields for harvesting certain fruits they need in the time between death and rebirth. If we follow dead souls with clairvoyant vision, we find that these fields which the dead need are sleeping human souls. Someone who first perceives this in the world of spirit will no doubt find it not only surprising but very poignant to see how human souls living between death and rebirth rush as it were toward sleeping human souls to seek for the thoughts and ideas they harbour. These nourish them, they need this sustenance. Each evening when we fall asleep, we can say that the ideas and thoughts that passed through our mind while we were awake, come alive, become, as it were, living beings. And the dead souls come to graze upon these meadows, to share in these ideas. Gazing upon them, they feel nourished. Oh indeed, it is harrowing and stirring when you observe clairvoyantly how those who have died pay nightly visits to the sleeping people they have left behind [...].[92]

Growing Old—a Challenge for Education

When does a life on earth begin and when does it end? We are involved in a continual process of evolution and transformation, many aspects of which have been described here. From the perspective of recurring lives on earth, there is continual alternation, comparable to a breathing rhythm or water cycle. Goethe, a thinker for whom reincarnation was a reality, wrote this:

The human soul
is like water:
it comes from heaven,
it rises to heaven;
and to earth again
it must return.[93]

Thus our life is bound up in a greater process: human development that starts with the education of the child finds only a provisional culmination in the life we live in old age. Nevertheless, or because of this, education has huge significance, potentially giving children a sense of their participation in a greater cosmic and spiritual context that lends meaning, and sets challenges, whose outcome will only be fully manifest in maturity or old age. This chapter, dealing with educational tasks that relate to healthy ageing, therefore first takes a look at our origins as human beings, the pre-existence for which Steiner, referring to pre-birth developmental processes, coined the term 'unbornhood'.

The art of education must draw its potency from a comprehensive evolutionary perspective. Reflecting on our origin in a pre-birth existence is a wellspring when considering ageing processes. An 'education for ageing' is the theme of the second part of the chapter. If children can develop a sense or intimation that they have come from a spiritual existence, and during the course of life can consolidate this thought into ever greater certainty, this will inwardly colour their whole life. Lacking this momentum, it is harder to find meaning in life, or find anything to set against the outward depletion and decline of forces in age. Resilience is a much-used term in modern gerontology: it indicates an inner capacity and strength to meet crises, and so to live on confidently into old age. The anthroposophic psychologist and pedagogue Johannes W. Schneider sums this up trenchantly in the sub-title for his book on ageing, *Growing old is not for cowards*.

When he founded Waldorf education, Rudolf Steiner gave a still far from exhausted impetus for new forms of teaching and learning. Education that includes a vision of ageing will always involve a reciprocal process: our experience in old age can also provide insights useful in education. The importance of a child's lifestyle and surroundings, of how we nurture a child, often only becomes apparent in their later life.

Unbornhood: the pre-birth journey

It would be mistaken to look only to the future and to see old age only in terms of what follows it, fixating perhaps on our desire for further lives on earth. Much that relates to our future can be understood properly only in terms of the past where we originate. In a lecture he gave in Dornach in 1921, Rudolf Steiner urged a reversal of perspective in order for us to observe our human existence with fewer preconceptions, with less egoism. Instead of thinking of 'immortality', he said, we should think of 'unbornhood', a term that he repeatedly emphasized. To delve into our human pre-existence in our thoughts and feelings, and to gain the insights into human life this can offer, was of great social and ethical significance for him.

When the idea of pre-existence was jettisoned from western culture, it was tantamount to dismissing selfless enquiry too. Those who preach immortality, as I have often said, are, basically, appealing to human egoism. Of course people feel uncomfortable at the thought of death, they fear life's cessation. Certainly, life does not end. But those who preach immortality do not address powers of knowledge and insight but are appealing to people's fear of death, their desire to go on living after they are deprived of a body. In other words, it is an appeal to egoism. This isn't the case when speaking of pre-existence. People today don't really give a fig about whether or not they lived previously before being born or conceived. What they care about is that they are alive now. So they are not much interested in pre-existence. Post-existence is what they are concerned with. Alive now, as they know themselves to be, they do not know whether there is a life after death, and this relates to their egoism. Unconsciously or instinctively—if they have not developed inner knowledge—they do not care whether or not they lived before being conceived or born, for now that they are alive what they want is to go on living.

This is the mood that basically underpins people's feelings of enthusiasm for immortality. And that is why, in all major languages we are familiar with, there is a word for immortality in reference to eternity after the end of life but not a word for 'unbornhood', for the life we have before being born. This is something we must slowly encourage. It is a term that addresses knowledge and understanding, that speaks more to a lack of egoism, to ego-free perception and study of the human being. And that is what we must appeal to. And altogether, knowledge and insight must be imbued with morality, with ethics. [94]

> In our enquiries into ageing, therefore, let us now look in the opposite direction, travelling backwards into the pre-birth period. In this way we meet the future individual as they surround themselves with the etheric body around the third week of pregnancy. In doing so, they experience something comparable to what happens when they pass through the portal of death: just as a panoramic vision of our past life unfolds before us then, the soul approaching birth gains a comprehensive 'picture of life's possibilities'. This prospect can be an occurrence that informs and colours the whole of their future life, as Rudolf Steiner described in his lecture on 6 June 1909.

At birth, when we return to the earth, we take a path that is the reverse of what happens at death. First the astral body incorporates itself, then the etheric body, and last of all the physical body. At death we first lay aside the physical body, then the etheric body and lastly the astral body.

And when we receive the etheric body, what happens resembles our passage through the portal of death when we had a panoramic vista of our past life. Now we have prophetic foresight or foreknowledge of the life on which we are embarking. This is highly significant for us and happens at the moment when the etheric body incorporates itself. This moment vanishes again from our memory. We do not see details but a picture or panorama of the possibilities life holds in store. This foreknowledge can only become calamitous if it gives us something like a shock or fright, or in other words we resist entering physical life. In ordinary circumstances the etheric body and physical body merge, but in these instances the shock means that they do not. Then the etheric body does not fully enter the physical body, but extends beyond it especially in the head region and then cannot properly elaborate the organs of thinking. Some cases of idiocy are caused by this, though, it must be emphasized, by no means all.[95]

> In the summer of 1919, Rudolf Steiner gave a singular account of something he had observed. He had noticed that in the years preceding the First World War, the features of arriving souls had changed in mood. Many of these souls appeared more troubled and seemed to find it hard to embark on life. There was a hindrance present, as if, said Steiner, they knew their ' "spiritual plumage" would be enmired' in the 'materialistic outlook' that awaited them.

Today I want to start with a phenomenon that is scarcely noticed amongst the tumultuous upheavals of our times, or if it is, is seen as something minor and unimportant. Yet it is signally present for those who have drawn from spiritual foundations the possibility of observing life in its full reality.

Somewhere between seven or eight and ten years ago—this may sound paradoxical but it is true—a keen observer of life will have noticed that children began to be born with very different expressions on their faces than before. People scarcely notice such things because they overlook life's most important phenomena. But those who have gained an eye for such things know that something troubled has been appearing in the features of children born over the past seven, eight or ten years, something like wariness of the world. We can notice this in their features from their earliest days, the first few weeks: there is something different in their expression from what used to be there. And if we study this remarkable fact—one that will seem paradoxical to modern people—we find that the souls of children bringing themselves into the world at birth, passing through conception and birth, carry with them something that lends their features almost from the moment of birth a melancholic expression, often even concealed under their smiles. This is something different from what you used to see on the faces of children. And in their souls, completely unconscious of course, lives something like a disinclination to enter life. The souls who come to birth today—as I say, this has been happening for almost ten years now—feel in some way blocked and hindered from entering this physical world.

Before we enter the physical world through conception and birth, we undergo an important occurrence in the world of spirit which then casts its rays forward into the life to come, and makes its influence felt there. People die here on earth, they cross the threshold of death, lay aside their physical body, bring their souls into the world of spirit. This soul bears within it still the effects of everything it has experienced here in the physical world. The soul, after passing through death, really appears like these effects themselves of what has been directly experienced here in earthly life. Now these souls who have crossed the threshold—this is a fact, and I can only describe what I myself have experienced of the world of spirit—encounter souls preparing to descend into a physical body in the near future. This encounter is an important occurrence: those who have just passed through death meet those who are soon to enter the physical world through the portal of birth. The encounter has a decisive effect and exists in a sense to inoculate descending souls with an idea of what they will meet here. And in this encounter originates the impulse that stamps this curious melancholy upon the features of newborn children. They do not want to come into the world they have learned of through this encounter, for they know that their 'spiritual plumage' will be enmired in what humanity, immersed as it is in a materialistic outlook, is going through today on earth. These—naturally only spiritually observable—occurrences help illuminate our whole modern era, which we can in turn only understand, and must try to understand, against such a backdrop.[96]

> In a lecture cycle which Steiner gave in Berlin in 1915 on the development of destiny, and life after death, he further described the encounter between souls who have just died and those just incarnating, in this case relating to souls who have died between the ages of 11 and 14.

If we trace the path of such a soul in the world of spirit, we find it relatively quickly in very particular company, if I can put it like that, at a particular period between death and rebirth: we find it amongst souls who are preparing for their next life and must soon descend to earth, thus amongst souls who will soon incarnate. Amongst these we find living the souls of those who crossed the threshold of death between the ages of 11 and 14. And if we take a closer look at their exchanges, curiously we discover that the souls who will soon descend to their life on earth need what these other souls can bring up to them from the earth in order to gain the strength they require to become embodied. These youthful souls therefore provide vigorous help to those who must soon come down to a life on earth. The kind of help given by these souls of perfectly ordinary children—who had no special mental or spiritual life but were simply alert and sprightly children—is one that can no longer be provided by those who die at a later age.[97]

> The path to birth is intentionally prepared over centuries. The conscious soul makes its way through the afterlife until, at the furthest remove from earth, a reversal occurs. The soul, or more aptly the human being's eternal self, experiences itself in intuitive consciousness as living within the other. With this reversal and the path of return to a new life on earth, as Steiner described in Berlin on 2 April 1918, the soul begins to feel an affinity with the future stream of generations. Intuitive consciousness helps the soul to immerse itself 'in what lives through generations'. When we are born, something characteristic echoes onward from our pre-birth period: this is the power of imitation whose underlying tenor characterizes infancy.

At a certain point in the life between death and rebirth, the soul begins to feel an affinity with the sequence of generations which will eventually lead to mother and father. Gradually the soul feels related to the ancestors as they are led to one another in marriages and have children. [...] Gradually one learns to perceive the thirty-sixth, thirty-fifth ancestral pair, then the thirty-fourth, thirty-third, thirty-second, all the way down to father and mother. One learns to discern this, woven into Imaginations, Intuition imprinting itself in this, until one arrives at father and mother. This imprinting is really a merging with what lives through the generations. The second half of the life between death and rebirth is such that we become deeply accustomed to living in the other, already prefiguring this other existence, the closer and wider environments as they will become—living not within oneself but in this otherness. Between death and rebirth we attend to this otherness, hearken to it, live primarily in it. Then we are born, and for a period we retain something from this other life. And this is why it has to be recognized that we are imitators in the first seven years of life; we imitate everything we perceive. Read my text on *The Education of the Child in the Light of Spiritual Science*. The first phase of childhood is a last echo of this 'living in the other' as it continues on into physical life. This quality and characteristic is the most excellent spiritual property we possess between death and rebirth, and is the first quality that appears in the child: imitation of everything that is there. We fail to understand this imitative capacity in the child if we do not know that it originates in the grandeur of the spirit-soul's intuitive life in the latter period of the life between death and rebirth.[98]

> Rudolf Steiner was in Kristiania—today's Oslo—at Whitsun 1923 for the founding of the Norwegian Anthroposophical Society. Nowhere else did he speak in such detail about the soul's path before birth. In the following excerpt from his lecture on 17 May 1923, he finds inspired words to describe the sublime work of creating a future human body that is performed by human souls together with divine beings.

But what I will call a 'celestial culture' accomplished between death and rebirth, when the human body is prepared, woven in spirit, is far more comprehensive in scope, a work far more grandiose than all earthly civilization. There is nothing more sublime in the cosmic order than weaving the human being from all the world's constituents. In the most important period between death and a new birth, the human being is woven in collaboration with gods.

Yesterday I said that the experiences we have here on earth, things we learn and acquire, are in a sense nourish-

ment for the cosmos. But equally it is true that having preserved in one life on earth the nourishment or fuel that is
useful to the cosmos, and having given it away to the cosmos,
we receive from the cosmos again all the substances from
which in turn to weave the new form into which we will later
be incorporated. Given up truly and entirely to a world of
spirit, we live then as spirit. Our whole being and activity is
spiritual work and spiritual existence. This lasts a long time.
It has to be continually reiterated that weaving human nature
is a truly mighty and majestic work. In the ancient mysteries,
the human body was rightly called the 'temple of the gods'.
This is a phrase of deep significance. Increasingly we learn to
feel its deep meaning the more we gain insight into the whole
of initiation science, into our human life itself between death
and rebirth. There we live as spirit beings in the very sight of
spirit beings, and this lasts for a long time, after which
another condition begins.[99]

> A similar lecture passage accentuates the balancing or
> redress of karma:

You see, everything you can accomplish on earth is not of
the grandeur and manifold nature of what you accomplish
when you form the human body, the 'temple of the gods'
out of the breadths of celestial worlds. That is far more
magnificent and complex work. You do not merely form
your own body, in fact, but as we will see in a moment,
you form it in a way that makes it, really, a part of all
humanity: your karma has brought you together with this
or that person, and now you form your new body such that
you endow it with qualities that enable it to relate rightly to
these other human beings, so that you can balance or
redress your karma with them. In other words, you work

for all humanity to a much greater degree than would be possible for you here on earth.[100]

> Once the new body has been formed, a new, individual life on earth can begin. The immortal, spiritual core of the human being, our true self, does not however accompany the earthly body's journey. In his lecture of 19 December 1915, Steiner addressed this difficult idea, and eight years later created a deep mantra on the same theme, that of the I which stops short and remains in the world of spirit.

And this is the mystery, hard to understand, that at the point where our memory begins, the time we can remember back to later in life, the I stops short: it does not alter as the body does, it stops. And it is precisely by virtue of this that we have it ever before us so that, as we look to it, it reflects our experiences back to us. The I does not accompany our earthly journey. Not until we cross the threshold of death and have to travel through kamaloka, back again to our birth, do we encounter our I once more, and then take it with us on our further journey. Our body presses forward through the years while our I remains behind, stays put. This is difficult to grasp because we cannot conceive of something stopping in time as time continues. Yet this is what happens. The I stops, and does so because this I does not actually connect with what approaches us from earthly existence, but instead remains connected, bound up, with the forces we call ours in the world of spirit. The I remains there, basically remains in the form which, as we know, is lent us by the spirits of form. This I is retained in the spiritual world, and if this were not so we could never attain our intrinsic and original task and goal as human beings on earth during earthly evolution. What we have undergone here on earth through our Adam nature, of which we bear an imprint into the grave when we die as Adam, adheres to the physical body, etheric body and astral body, and comes from these. The I waits, waits with everything within it, throughout the time we spend on earth, only gazes upon the person's further development; and we gather it to us again after passing through the portal of death and taking the return path. In other words, we remain with our I—and I mean this in a particular sense—in the spiritual world. Humanity should develop awareness of this, an awareness that is only possible because the Christ descended at a certain point from worlds, worlds of spirit to which the human being belongs, and—in a twofold way, as we have heard—prepared in the body of Jesus what was to serve him as body upon the earth.

If we understand ourselves aright, we gaze back to our childhood throughout our life on earth, to where our spiritual being has remained. If we have a proper understanding of these things, we always look back to this. And humankind should be educated to look to this, to have a proper sense and vision of the intrinsic quality of which the spirit from the heights can say, 'Suffer the little children to come unto me.'[101]

Meditation to find the I

> I look into the dark:
> within it arises light,
> living light.
> Who is this light in the dark?
> I am it myself in my reality.
> This reality of the I
> does not enter my earthly life.

I am only an image of it.
But I will find it once again
when, with good will for the spirit,
I have passed beyond death's gate.[102]

> When we know of the soul's pre-existence, the course of life
> on earth also acquires a different significance for us. Above
> all, birth and infancy come to have a different worth.
> Understanding our spiritual origin is of particular relevance
> for education. We need a pedagogy that takes account of
> this, by means of which young people can feel themselves to
> be part of a greater, meaningful context. Only when they are
> inwardly imbued with such meaning, says Rudolf Steiner on
> 21 January 1921, does a capacity grow in them that enables
> them to meet the impotence of modern times with 'socially
> active strength'. Seeds that thrive on such a soil will bring
> rich harvests in their mature years.

If rightly understood, this conscious insight into the pre-
existence of the soul would not remain merely theoretical but
would take hold of people's feeling and will and thus grow to
be real strength in life.

Look at modern people: they all show a lack of broader
initiative to some degree. This lack of initiative in larger
matters, which has such a debilitating effect on all the forces
that would be required to turn decline into ascent, is a
paralysis that can only improve if people become fully aware
that they are part of a world of spirit.[103]

If children grew up under the influence of a world view such as
this, they would feel themselves to be a part of the cosmos, and
draw strong feelings of life from forces they would imbibe by
apprehending the cosmos. In being brought up to act, too,
they would know that whatever they did was imprinted into

the whole universe. If this feeling of things developed, how differently people would live from how they do today, when they can so easily ask themselves what their life is worth as lonely entities sprung from vague forces of nature, in whom moral ideals surface and burst like soap bubbles. With this outlook people's sense of life is so easily paralysed. They look up to the starry breadths and see the planets wandering through space, but have no real relationship to all this, for they regard themselves only as naturally arising and disintegrating worlds without meaning or inward spirituality. [...]

Anthroposophy seeks to provide a science imbued with spirit, one that enlivens people. What filters through to us as a perception of the spirit in nature is transformed in the human being into social energy, just as, physically, food is transformed within our digestive system. If people sought to attend fully to this, they would recognize that spirit knowledge is absorbed and digested as food for the soul, and is released in turn as socially effective energy. We will only gain the social impulses we need if we absorb spiritual insights from surrounding nature. To think that social reforms will come from any other source is more or less equivalent to thinking that withholding all food from someone amounts to a healthy diet. If you speak of social reforms and not, at the same time, of spiritual insights, you treat the social order like someone to whom you deny food in the misguided belief that this is healthy. That is how absurd modern people's outlooks are, but they fail to see it.[104]

Suggestions for upbringing and education

The first passage in this section shows clearly that Steiner regarded the Waldorf impulse as an answer to cultural

decline and demise at the beginning of the twentieth century. At that period, many people felt that the 'times were
changing', apparent in major cultural upheavals. Steiner
repeatedly pointed to these symptoms, seeing his work as
serving the emergence of a new era.

It is evident that the old has to die to give way to the new.
This became apparent in all areas of society at the start of the
twentieth century. On 10 October 1916, midway through
the war years, Steiner gave a lecture in Zurich entitled 'How
Can We Overcome Soul Adversity?'

People will find it ever more difficult, as this fifth post-
Atlantean age continues, to gain the right relationship to each
other, since this actually requires inner development, inner
exertion, inner activity. These difficulties have begun but they
will deepen and spread, become ever more acute. Today even
people whom karma brings together find it hard to directly
understand one another because, perhaps, other karmic circumstances mean they do not find the strength to be
instinctively aware of all the connections that exist from former
incarnations. People are led to one another, love one another,
and this derives from certain effects in previous incarnations.
But other forces counteract this: a reminiscence surfaces and
they part again. It is not just people who encounter each other
like this in life, who have to discover whether what rises in them
in response to the other is really sufficient to establish a lasting
relationship. It is also growing ever harder for sons, daughters,
mothers and fathers to understand each other; it is increasingly
difficult for parents to understand their children, or for siblings
to understand one another. Mutual understanding will
become increasingly difficult since it will be more and more
necessary for people to allow the karma that resides in them
really to surface from within.

So you can see the negative perspective that will unfold over the course of the fifth post-Atlantean era: problems in mutual understanding between people. But this means we must look this evolutionary condition square in the face, rather than trying to dream our way through it in the dark. The consciousness soul could not develop, and we would have to live in natural, instinctive community, without this problematic destiny hanging over humanity in the fifth post-Atlantean epoch—without these difficulties in knowing one another. The individualizing character of the consciousness soul could not otherwise develop. So we have to go through these trials. But at the same time we must look this reality squarely in the face, for if only this negative aspect of evolutionary conditions in the fifth post-Atlantean era were to emerge, then of course war and conflict would reign and would work their way right into the closest relationships. We can see a sum of instinctive needs emerging in this fifth post-Atlantean epoch, but these must be configured and shaped in ever more conscious ways. Doing so is one of the tasks of spiritual science for the humanity of this fifth post-Atlantean age.[105]

Today there are already enough people whose hearts bleed to see these conditions—which, though necessary, will only take effect in the right way if we fully understand them. The impulses for new universal action must be consciously drawn from our heart's blood. What arises by itself is alienation of individuals from each other, and in response we must consciously endeavour to let flow what is needed from human hearts. Difficulties await every single soul in the fifth post-Atlantean epoch, and only by overcoming them will we meet and engage with the trials through which the consciousness soul can be developed.[106]

For alienation, especially between the generations, to be overcome, we need insight into the singularity of the nature of the child. This gains all the more significance when we recognize that our character in later years, and the manner in which we mature, is laid down in childhood. The foundations established in childhood through education and upbringing, go on working; in fact, they often only manifest in later years, whether negatively or positively. On Michaelmas Day 1923, Rudolf Steiner spoke of the great responsibility borne by parents, carers and educators.

It is true to say that what may manifest in someone in, say, earliest infancy, often remains concealed for a long time and only assumes distinctive form in advanced old age, and then shows itself either as morbid or health-giving. As parents and educators, not only the child before us but the whole of a human life on earth lies in our hands. [...] What the soul acquires in childhood works down into the depths of the soul and only comes to expression in old age—and can then be a power that emanates blessing.[107]

All teaching of children should be done in a way that makes it a source of rejuvenation throughout a person's life, said Steiner on 19 January 1918 in Berlin, during a lecture cycle entitled *Dying Earth and Living Cosmos*. Here he touches the nerve of what is involved in healthy ageing: the maturation process that begins in youth must continue on into the most advanced old age. Providing the right foundations for such lifelong learning and support is not an endeavour of anthroposophic pedagogy only, but something that is coming to the fore also in modern gerontology (see the last chapter in this book, page 213).

For the 'sustenance' that young people receive through their upbringing and education to last a lifetime, Steiner says, we need a 'fuller and richer head knowledge' than modern education usually provides. Only in this way can we avoid an education at risk of producing acerbic and prematurely old people.

Consider what it means for a person to really feel themselves integral to cosmic contexts, not a mere product of the physical aspects of space and time but a part of huge dimensions. It is very striking to see—not only as Goethe did when he saw the skull bones as a metamorphosis of the vertebrae—how everything in the human head can be rediscovered elsewhere in the human organism. But to develop an eye for this we need a mode of observation devoid of preconceptions—so as to see not only the nose and everything upon the head as a metamorphosis but also everything in the rest of our organism in terms of a more recent, a younger metamorphosis. All this is reconfigured in an older metamorphosis in what then appears in the human head.

As I said, the consequences of such an outlook are extraordinarily important pedagogically; and if human thinking eventually comes to embrace spiritual-scientific insights this will be hugely beneficial also for matters of practical pedagogy.

One thing above all is important: we grow old, that is part of life. But actually we can only say that our physical body grows old. As strange as it may seem—and I have mentioned this before—our etheric body, the adjoining and first spiritual aspect of our being, grows ever younger. The older we become, the younger does our etheric body grow. While our physical body gets wrinkles, goes bald, our etheric body flourishes, or can do so, can grow ever 'chubbier-cheeked'. But whereas outward nature ensures that our physical body grows older, we ourselves must ensure that youthful forces keep flowing to our etheric body. And we can only do so if we introduce through the head the food of spiritual ideas of a kind sufficient to go on being assimilated throughout life.

A spiritual-scientific observer finds such sustenance in the way in which one might teach a young child how the human being is an image of the whole universe, an image of the divine, wise cosmic order. But this must be offered in a manner that can be grasped directly, in elementary form rather than by inculcating the child with uncomprehended words from the Bible. It must be summoned in the spirit of spiritual science, and then it will engender a richer, fuller head knowledge than we have today. And then it will become a fount of rejuvenation throughout the child's whole life. Our modern education is no such fount, but the opposite. If we are fortunate enough today not to have become terribly acerbic because of our early education, this is only because the modern way of addressing the head—which has been developing over the past four hundred years—has not yet been able to wreck the inherited culture that does still, after all, remain from olden times. But if we go on teaching in a way that only addresses the head, we will be in the greatest danger of educating people to be terribly sour and acerbic in their later years.[108]

> In 1922, young people and students asked Rudolf Steiner to discuss with them the gulf between the generations and what it meant to be young. For two weeks he gave lectures to around 80 young people, and held individual and group discussions with them. This intense and intimate encounter was also concerned with what must be kindled in young souls in order to give them perspectives for the future and make their mature years seem worth striving for.

> As part of the youth course on education, in a lecture on
> 12 October 1922 Rudolf Steiner described the strong inner
> need he perceived in young people for attention and
> understanding from older people: only through such
> encounters between young and old, he said, would their
> awakening I be consolidated. They sought people with life
> experience in whom they could believe, without having such
> faith forcibly imposed on them. It was important to
> reawaken the sense that they could learn something from
> older people that would help them in their own inner quest.

To understand youth as opposed to age we must enter into
the intimacies of the art of education. Mere phrases will not
do. The gulf between youth and age must be bridged through
an art of education that does not shy away from embracing
real spiritual-scientific insight. A few days ago I asked what is
involved in this art of education. It is concerned with an
experience of the reality of the spirit. And what, by contrast,
has gradually come to be the focus of our era, and seen as
intrinsic to the education of the young? Not spirit, but its lack
or absence! Nowadays it is thought to be a sin to 'muddy' the
clear waters of knowledge and science with spirit.

Even in infancy this science does not leave children
untouched. It is hardly surprising, for if one has been trained,
say, in botanical classification systems, a teacher will think it
a sin to speak to children in any other way. But a child before
the age of ten can make nothing of such botany. Only around
the age of 18 or so can they form a relationship with it.

Now I do not want what I say to be rendered in turn into
another intellectual theory about education. An artistic
atmosphere needs to be created between adults and the
young. Only if this happens can young people today grow
into the world around them in a sound and healthy way. It is

possible to describe very tangibly what people today are growing into. Between the age of about 8 and 9, a vague feeling lives in the soul of every person as long as they are not a psychopath. It need not be formulated as a clear thought, it may not even be a vague thought, but it starts to live in a person from the age of 8 or 9. Until that point what we call the astral body has taken care of the child's soul life by itself, but from that point onward the power of our I nature starts to stir in us. This I nature is not formulated in thought. But in feeling, in a deeply unconscious form in the soul, a question stirs in the sensibility of the growing child. This question will assume diverse forms depending on the person. To conceptualize it we could say something like this: hitherto the astral body believed in other people; but now I need something that someone tells me so that I can believe in them or in various people around me. The children who most reject such a thing in fact need it most. Between the age of 8 and 9 we start to need to have our I consolidated through a belief in an older person. We must be able to believe in this person without this belief being imposed or inculcated. We have to be able to believe in someone through the artistic atmosphere that has been created. And woe betide us if no adult does anything to truly answer this unspoken question—one that can linger on in some children until they are 15 or 16, even in some cases until they are 17 or 18. If on the other hand children find an answer in the adults around them, they feel a sense of gratitude for this experience. They sense that the person who gave them this response could only have done so now, and that if they met with it later, as adults, its nature would have changed.

In turn, something can be created in consequence in a pedagogical manner which, properly applied, can be of the

greatest significance for the age of the consciousness soul—
something that was already playing between young and old in
the most ancient times of the patriarchs. In those days every
young person knew that an ancient with snow on his head
possessed experiences that they could only have once they
had grown as old as he was. Prior to this they knew they did
not have the necessary organs of understanding, and so an
ancient must tell them his experiences; and their connection
with his words was due to his particular experiences and
qualities. Though they would one day grow as old as such an
ancient, they knew they would have to wait 35 or 40 years
before experiences such as his were granted them, though by
then time would have moved on, and so their experiences
would be different ones.

In the deep strata of world culture lies something like a
chain of links that extend from the past to the future, and
which successive generations must take up, continue, forge
and develop further. But this chain has been ruptured in the
intellectualistic era. At the turn of the nineteenth to the
twentieth century, young people universally felt this. Do you
feel that you felt something like this back then, even if you
could not express it at the time? Try to feel about this in the
right way! If you feel and sense it, you will experience the real
significance of today's youth movement, which has a Janus
head—looking both backward and forward—and must have,
because it seeks and needs an experience of the spirit, one
that pursues a train of thought far enough to turn it into will,
into the most inward human impulse.[109]

> The dialogue between the generations gives young people
> an opportunity to see themselves as whole human beings.
> Unconsciously, many young people certainly have a sense of

coming from worlds of spirit. As Steiner says in his lecture on 22 January 1921, there is no need to inform them of this. The task of the older generation, of teachers of the young, is not to inculcate children with knowledge but to remove obstacles that impede their own developing insights. But to do this we need a deeper understanding of the child: educators must see themselves as midwives in a sense.

Some children today are born with different spiritual capacities. The term 'indigo' or 'rainbow' children is simply a way of expressing certain qualities that these children bring with them at birth, and which Steiner, in his own day, already acknowledged.

Today we live in an era that follows an evolutionary turning point, a radical change. What people previously learned between birth and death through the mysteries, they learn today before they descend into a physical body through conception and birth. They learn it in correspondence with their karma, following preparations for it in a former life on earth. Thus the experience we undergo between the great midnight hour of existence and rebirth includes and encompasses this learning. [...]

We have to assume something like this when we encounter the child. Education is no longer a matter of inculcating children with things imparted to them in ancient times. Instead we must recognize that children have already received this instruction before clothing their instructed souls in a physical body. Thus we need to reach through this outer sheath and draw forth the pre-birth instruction of the gods. That is the modern pedagogical approach. If we truly embrace anthroposophically oriented spiritual science, it is clear that in education we can really do nothing other than remove obstacles that impede the emergence of what children bring with them into the world from their pre-birth existence. This is why we place such infinite importance in our Waldorf pedagogy on teachers observing the child as a riddle that they need to decipher, approaching what is concealed within. Certainly it is not of primary importance to inculcate children with whatever subject matter teachers think necessary. They must never proceed dogmatically but must regard children themselves as their teachers. [...]¹¹⁰

> Rudolf Steiner repeatedly stressed how important it is to sufficiently educate school children's feelings and sensibility. 'If we open ourselves to life in this way in our youth, life will go on opening up more and more later on.' These words of Steiner's on 7 January 1911—years still before the founding of the Waldorf school—can be seen not only as a guiding motif for school education but also as a vital contribution to preventing age-related decline or, more accurately, to supporting healthy maturation and ageing. As opposed to the enlivening effect of feelings nurtured and cultivated in youth, too much 'rationality' leads the young soul to be 'prematurely elderly'. A form of teaching that seeks to be pictorial develops the sensibility and feelings. Nowadays, increasingly, people cite the need for 'emotional intelligence' and the empathic capacity. Nurturing such qualities is intrinsic to Waldorf education.

If we notice this kind of wide-ranging sensibility in someone, a sensibility of broad compass, we find that they will stay young for a long time, young at heart, even when their hair goes grey. They retain a certain flexibility or mobility. In particular they will retain throughout their lives an ability to adjust rapidly to different situations, to be skilful in handling them. If we open ourselves to life in this way in our youth, life will go on opening up more and more later on. We become ever more able to develop insights, and find it easier to sense the spirit underlying things. We become ever more spiritual. This is different from someone who especially developed their rational side in youth. Such people tend to grow prematurely old. This isn't the fault of any individual but the communal karma of society. A very rational person increasingly sunders themselves from the world, which seems to them ever more incomprehensible. This is why many criticize everything around them. In my youth—they say—everything was lovely but now it's been ruined. This morose quality, this unhappiness with everything, this withdrawal into childhood memories, is connected with the soul's excessive rationality in youth. This is why it is so important to do everything we can to nurture a broad and encompassing sensibility, particularly by founding education on pictorial imagination.

Nowadays, humanity in general is heading straight for the very opposite of this. It is thought wrong to 'lie' to children that babies are brought by the stork. Actually this is just a picture, but one containing more truth than the 'factual information' people try to impress on children today— that the child comes from father and mother alone. The image of the stork—or other such images—points to the aspect of the child that descends from lofty heights. Through such an image the child gazes up into regions beyond mundanity, and creates a foundation for what will later emerge as truth. To see the tale of the stork as untrue just testifies to lack of imagination, an inability to find an apt picture in which to clothe the processes of reincarnation, which it would be wrong to speak of directly to the child. People object that children no longer believe such tales. But this is because the adults who tell them to children nowadays do not themselves believe in what the pic-

ture expresses, and so the children can't believe it either.
But if we know it to be an image of underlying reality, and
if we have enough imagination to transform reality into pictures, children will believe us. It is in fact a beautiful thing
to tell a child that father and mother both do their part, but
that a third element is brought down by other beings from
celestial heights, who bear it on their wings to father and
mother. Such a picture is very apt and accurate: it is true.
We nurture children's astral life by imparting to them rich,
vivid pictures, and we give them the blessing of a youthfulness that reaches far into their later years. This pictorial
quality in teaching, which also lives above all in their play,
is infinitely important. Here too we can see the effect of
karma even in a single life.

When spiritual science engages in culture it helps life to
thrive and flourish and reveal its truth, whereas materialism
demonstrates its untruth in the fact that life withers on the
vine and grows old prematurely.[111]

> The word 'mindfulness' is all the rage at present. People are
> receptive to this idea, which has also found its way into many
> classrooms. Let us hope that this is not simply a passing fad,
> for at its heart is an old and important tenet of education.
> The 'Pedagogical Province'—a rural educational institute
> that figures in Goethe's novel *Wilhelm Meister*—highlighted
> the importance of a threefold reverence. In 1921, likewise,
> in his 'Introduction to Anthroposophic Pedagogy and
> Didactics', known as the Christmas Course for Teachers,
> Steiner emphasized the importance of reverence as a fun-
> damental stance in the encounter between child and adult. If
> children can develop this authentic feeling, so that it 'lives
> on in them as a fundamental tenor of life', in their mature
> years it re-emerges as a special gift: the power to bless.

For those, particularly, who want to practise the art of education, this ability to enter into the flow of time is of great importance. Certain examples can illustrate this.

Let us assume that a child develops particular reverence for adults. If we have a sound sensibility, we will see it as a healthy thing if the child, with guidance, develops this kind of self-evident respect and reverence for the adult—as long as this reverence is justified by the qualities the adult actually possesses. We will speak further of this in further lectures on the art of education and teaching. For now I will cite just one example.

Usually people see no further than the moment and simply acknowledge that there are children who develop this quality or attribute of reverence. But we will never gain insight into the whole significance of such reverence without considering the whole of a person's life. If we contemplate the whole of life, however, and observe the child much later, in old age, we will find that there are people who have the singular, authentic, natural quality of comforting others who need comfort, or of offering encouragement and affirmation to others who need this, perhaps when they are in distress. Very often it is not the actual content of what these comforters and encouragers say to someone: it is, rather, something in the timbre of their voice, the very tone and way in which they speak. And if we look back through the life of such a person, we will find they were especially wedded to a quality of reverence in their childhood, to a deep respect for adults. This reverence for older people fades over time but lives on in the depths of a person's life, and in mature age re-emerges as the gift of offering solicitous encouragement, of raising others' spirits.

What I have here described from one perspective can also

be expressed as follows: we can say that if a child has learned really to pray inwardly, has learned to cultivate a mood of prayer, during the middle phase of life this prayerful mood goes underground but re-emerges in advanced old age. It comes to expression then as the particular gift of bringing blessing to others, something which others feel and experience. And those whose very presence in old age emanates blessing for those around them will be found to have absorbed and developed a mood of prayer in their youth. We only discover these things if we learn to live with time, to encompass a whole lifetime, in the same way that we are used to knowing space. It would be important for people to develop a knowledge that lives with time more immediately and does not simply draw conclusions about time through spatial conditions—as we do with clocks, for instance.[112]

> In two further lectures, Steiner describes specifically how this comes about.

If a teacher succeeds in this way in being a self-evident authority for a child—so that for instance we absorb something at the age of 8 or 9, take it on the authority of a beloved teacher—then moments will arrive in later life, perhaps when we're 45 or 50, when what we absorbed back then, or took on trust, surfaces again in our maturity. It will have slumbered below in the soul for decades, but now it surfaces again, and we encounter it with mature experience. And this is hugely fruitful in life: it is the stirring of inner life forces.[113]

Something quite different must come to pass: especially as teachers and educators we must fill our souls with the feeling, the awareness, that something mysteriously internalizes itself in the child, and therefore we must impart to children's feeling sensibility much that will only become comprehensible to them in their later life, which they will then be able to draw from their memory, and recall having heard and absorbed. Only then, they will realize, are they wise enough to understand many things. Nothing in future will have a sounder and more health-giving effect on human life than this ability of people to draw much sustenance from memories of what they were told and taught as children, which they only later come to understand.

If a person's life can unfold in this way, so that they draw forth from memory what they could not yet understand at the time, this will become a fount of healthy inner life. It will keep at bay the aridity that nowadays infects people's sensibility, that makes them feel hollow, so that they end up as sanatoria patients looking for something to be given them from outside themselves since their own souls are empty—because their education failed to give them riches which they could later recall and draw upon.[114]

> In a lecture on 11 April 1924, during a course on *The Essentials of Education* in Stuttgart, Steiner urged that education be regarded as something that acknowledges the full scope of our part in evolving humanity. The profession of teaching, he said, would only become a consecrated endeavour if we could see the human being as a microcosm within, and related to, the macrocosm. If this could come about, it would found social community 'in the true sense of the word'. At the end of this passage he sums up his thoughts on the theme in a meditative verse.

If a human being is properly educated on earth, the celestial human being is also rightly educated, for in the earthly human being lives the heavenly one. If we educate earthly human beings properly, through the little step forward they must take between birth and death, we also advance the heavenly human being in the right way.

But this takes due account of an outlook that rightly seeks knowledge of the cosmos, a knowledge aware that the human being is called to collaborate on building the great, spiritual edifice of the cosmos, which then also manifests in the sense world. If we rightly understand the task of education, it involves seeing that we collaborate in developing humanity, that we help build and shape it. [. . .]

Just as the visible world is reflected in the eye, so the whole human being is an eye of spirit, soul and body, in which the whole world is mirrored. This mirror image is not something we can perceive from without; we must experience it inwardly. Then it will not remain appearance, like an external reflection, but will become inner reality. In education, in consequence, the world will become human, and human beings will find themselves in the world. If we work educationally in this way, we can really feel how humanity is fragmented when all human experience dedicates itself to matter, and this is because souls do not enhance each other but lose one another through what is, in fact, a self-repudiation. If instead we turn to the spirit, what can be found in the spirit leads us to others. Social community in the true sense of the word must be founded in the spirit. Human beings must find themselves in the spirit, then one person can unite with another; and the world must be seen in the human being if human deeds are to build and create worlds. [. . .]

And now, to conclude, allow me to sum up what I have been speaking of, what I have been tending toward, in the following words:

Dedicating yourself to matter
means crushing souls.

Meeting in the spirit
means uniting human beings.

Beholding yourself in the human being
means building worlds.[115]

The Cosmological Dimension of Ageing

Human ageing, various aspects of which have been considered in these excerpts, is part of a more comprehensive
process, as was suggested in Chapter 1: the ageing of the
world itself, and of the whole cosmos. These aspects, the
cosmological dimension, will now be examined in more
detail. Just as we human beings age and die, the earth also
ages. And the eternal core of the human being, our
entelechy which survives death, will also survive the
earth's demise, and will pass on into a new future. But for
this to happen, earth's transitory nature must be pervaded
by new, living seeds, by forces of renewal and rebirth.
This calls on the response of each single individual. It is
up to each one of us whether to bring to maturity and
ripeness the seeds laid in our youth, and whether to offer
the cosmos sustenance through our wakeful spirit activity.
This has been within the scope of human freedom since
our I was equipped with the capacity of thinking. And thus
responsibility for the future of the cosmos likewise lies
with us.

In former times there were people versed in 'heavenly
lore' who understood the language of the stars, and could
read the script of planetary and stellar motions, which gave
direct expression to divine wisdom. For the sake of human
freedom, this connection with the world of gods had to be
ruptured. At the same time, the divine spark of the I awoke
in human beings. Truly living thinking is rooted in the
human being and extends upward to divine wisdom. Here a
new communion of the human being with the spirit world
develops, of a kind not previously possible. Rudolf Steiner
encapsulated this in a verse—here prefacing the next sec-

tion—which he wrote for his wife Marie Steiner-von Sivers at Christmas 1922.

At the end of this chapter, in a sense as future prospect, is an indication of the close connection of our evolving humanity with Christ knowledge. As the sun shines its radiant light upon all parts of the globe, and on all people, the Christ penetrates with his power all growth and decline both in human beings and the cosmos. Through spiritual science we can gain a relationship with this power of Christ not only through religious faith but informed by insight and perception. This will give deep understanding of existence, offering us a confident perspective on life far beyond ageing and death.

The ageing of the earth and the mission of human beings

Stars once spoke to us,
their silence now is world destiny;
awareness of this silence
can cause us earthly human beings pain.

But in mute stillness ripens
what we speak to the stars;
awareness of this speech
can strengthen our spiritual core.[116]

On New Year's Eve 1922, Steiner spoke in the Goetheanum about our human collaboration with the divine, spiritual realm. His lecture to members of the Anthroposophical Society culminated in words about the renewal that comes to us from such communion. He also described this form of spiritual experience as cultivating a 'cosmic rite'.

Our active, human thoughts are not intrinsically or naturally present on earth: they work and dwell in an organism which, through its state of equilibrium, is independent of outward nature. If we realize these autonomous thoughts, we give the earth a future. But for this purpose we must first possess them, these independent thoughts, since all the thoughts we form about nature in ordinary science are dying ones, are mere thought reflections, are not realities. The thoughts we absorb from spiritual enquiry, on the other hand, are enlivened in Imagination, Inspiration, Intuition. If we absorb them, then they become configurations that lead an independent existence in earthly life.

Writing of this kind of creative thinking in my little booklet on Goethe's worldview, I said that such thinking embodies the spiritual form of communication within humanity. When we give ourselves up to thoughts that only mirror outward nature, we merely repeat the past, live in corpses of the divine. But when we ourselves enliven our thoughts, we connect through our own being—communicate, receive communion—with the divine spirit that pervades the world and assures its future.

Thus spiritual knowledge is true communion, the beginning of a cosmic rite that accords with modern humanity, a culture that can grow by virtue of the fact that we now perceive how we inform our physical, mineral and vegetable organism with our astral and I organism, and how, by enlivening the spirit within us, we can also impress the spirit into what otherwise surrounds us as dead and dying nature.[117]

> The following day, Steiner described exactly how this happens. The cosmos receives the fruits of human deeds, which

are its sustenance. The celestial worlds depend on this so that 'the cosmos can continue'. In precise terms, Steiner here described the transition into the sun realm that we enter as purely spiritual beings.

It is here that we give up to the cosmos, as sustenance for it, everything that belongs not to our moral values but to what the gods have allowed us to experience on earth, that is useful to the cosmos and enables it to continue. Yes, it is really so: if we were to regard the cosmos as a machine—and as you know, I certainly do not see the cosmos as a machine, I am speaking metaphorically—then what we bring with us, after laying down our little package in the moon realm, would be like fuel in the sun region which we give to the ongoing cosmos, like the fuel that powers a machine.

And so we enter the realm of the world of spirit—for it is the same to say we enter the sun realm, or that we enter the world of spirit.[118]

> In his lectures, Rudolf Steiner spoke in various ways of the ageing process of both humanity and the earth, and described the capacity of spiritual science to have a rejuvenating effect.

There is no doubt that in our time humanity as a whole has grown old; it no longer in general has the youthfulness that it possessed in mythological times. Spiritual science must become an elixir of youth again for people, so that they can feel themselves to be pupils of existence throughout their lives.[119]

Many people today speak of the 'spirit'. But you who are absorbing spiritual science should be people who do not let themselves be distracted by mere talk of spiritual things. You should recognize the difference between mere words about spirit and attempts, founded on anthroposophy, to actually describe the world of spirit—accounts in which this world of spirit is described in as much detail as outward descriptions of the physical world of the senses. [...]

I wanted to say this to you today to underline the seriousness that should imbue our whole relationship with the culture of anthroposophy. You see, humanity's future evolution will in a real sense depend on how human beings today regard this relationship. If what I have described today is seen as the great majority of the world's people regard it, then Ahriman, when he comes, will be a dire and unwelcome guest for humankind. But if people can find the inner activity to consciously assimilate the things we have been considering today, to govern and direct them as is necessary for humanity to retain its freedom in the face of the power of Ahriman, then, when Ahriman appears, humanity will learn from him precisely what it needs to: will recognize that the earth must in fact enter upon its decline, but that precisely because of this, humanity will raise itself above and away from earthly existence. Once we reach a certain age in physical life our body degenerates, but we do not—if we're sensible—complain about its frailty, since we know that our soul is approaching a life that does not run parallel to this physical body, is not subsumed by it. In humanity there lives something that is not bound up with the earth's decline—which has already begun—but that grows ever more spiritual precisely because the earth is entering upon its physical decadence. Let us learn to say this unhesitatingly: Yes, indeed, the earth is in decline, and so is human life as far as its physical manifestation is concerned. But this itself can give us the strength to infuse our civilization with something that must live on immortally in all earth evolution through humanity even as the earth heads toward its demise.[120]

> It is clear from the lecture of 12 October 1919, that Steiner regards the change and transformation of which he speaks as a whole new paradigm, one whose radical change of consciousness recalls the transition from medieval times to the modern era. The predominant value in our age—that 'money rules the world'—has reached a limit, and it is becoming increasingly clear that materialistic thinking has no potential to inaugurate the necessary social renewal.

Small cultural shifts will not do it. We must square up to the fact that only great cultural impulses can sustain the further progress of humanity in future. We will need to summon our inner strength to really absorb new impulses. We must have the courage to impress upon people what it means to say that the earth has grown decadent, is in decline, and that what has sustained civilization until now, along with our habits and customs, is likewise involved in this decline. But out of this decline we should rescue a new spirituality that can be taken over with us into other worlds. [. . .].

If we go on clinging only to small shifts and minor remedies, if we do not labour to impress on humanity the need for a new culture of the spirit, we will not accomplish what is necessary. This is the only reliable starting point for a new social culture. Then, instead of social dynamics governed by economic factors, economic activity governed by and proceeding from the spirit will alone give rise to social community. We must recognize that the 'economic type' is finished, and that another type of human being must come: citizens of the world who are aware that they are constituted of more than just earthly heredity, that the forces of sun and moon and the starry heavens, forces of the supersensible world also live in them. In forms that people can understand, we must impress this upon them, and only this will enable humanity to make progress. Merely giving vent to nebulous mystical teachings is of no use whatsoever. Our mysticism must be true culture, active, spiritual culture.[121]

> The human being must become a 'co-creator in the cosmos', as Steiner again highlighted in his lecture of 23 March 1923.

Characteristic of our current state as human beings is that, in our inmost soul, we grow together with the earth through our thinking. But on the other hand this also means it is possible for us now, in the fifth post-Atlantean epoch, to send back to the cosmos thoughts which—as we described yesterday at the end of the lecture—we enliven within us through our life on earth.

Human beings descend from the heavenly to the earthly realm until they are fully on the earth. But what is our condition then? In fact, it is as if the earth were a mirror for us. We are not meant to simply go on growing downward into and below the earth. Thoughts in their dead element penetrate the earth, grasp what is dead, which belongs only to the earth element. But our own nature is such that, if we enliven our thoughts, we send them out like mirror images into the cosmos. In other words, everything that arises in us as living thoughts can be seen by the gods to shine back to them from the evolving human being. We are called to be co-creators in the cosmos, and asked to enliven our thoughts—for these thoughts are reflected back by the earth and return out into the universe, must make their way back into the cosmos again.

If we absorb the whole meaning of human and world evolution then we can feel how we return in a particular way to the epochs we passed through previously. In Egyptian-Chaldean times, people calculated how things are for human beings on earth, though this calculation always connected human beings with the surrounding world of stars. Nowadays we do this in historical terms, starting from the human being as the point of departure for observations such as you find in my *Occult Science, an Outline,* where in fact we send forth enlivened human thoughts again and attend to what happens to them as we trace them, as it were, in their flight away from us in the cosmic environment, and learn to live in cosmic breadths with these enlivened thoughts.[122]

Becoming ever more human, and knowledge of Christ

Every person today can become a co-creator of the cosmos, though the old forms in which this was once done have been superseded. All ancient cultures were rooted in values that originated in a direct interplay and collaboration between human beings and gods. The leaders of humanity assimilated knowledge, the messages of the gods, through Inspiration, and people lived directly in this 'primordial wisdom'. Only when there was a danger of this connection rupturing were the sacred teachings written down and passed on in the books of wisdom of diverse cultures.

Today, esteem for this traditional wisdom of ancient cultures is fading. The Latin and Greek classics for instance, are vanishing from the educational canon. Repeatedly in his lectures, Rudolf Steiner speaks of the decline of that direct connection with the world of spirit, and of the need to gain

supersensible knowledge by new means. As decline takes
hold, the new is already germinal.

Decline and demise are natural processes. Just as we cannot remain children as we mature but gradually enter upon
a process of ageing, so all of humanity has embarked upon
a downward trajectory. We have left the fourth epoch
behind us and are now in the fifth; together with this fifth
era, the sixth and seventh will represent the ever more
elderly state of present world evolution. To think that old
ideals can be perpetuated is as clever as thinking that a person should spend their whole life learning their letters, or
learning to spell, because it is good for children to do
so.[123]

But this primordial wisdom must gradually dry up, and
something new, in the form of insights into the world of
spirit, must be achieved. For this to happen, though, human
beings must show some willingness to adopt things that
directly lead toward really new ideas. Modern humanity
needs new ideas, especially when it comes to matters of the
soul. Academic or scientific teachings about the soul and
psyche today are basically only words.[124]

Nowadays it is necessary for people to recognize that we
gain knowledge of nature, on the one hand, and on the
other, supersensible knowledge. Understanding of nature,
as such, is devoid of moral impulses, which have to be
gained through a knowledge that is supersensible. And
since, ultimately, social impulses must also be moral ones,
true social insight, or even just a sum of social impulses, is
inconceivable unless we raise ourselves to supersensible
knowledge.[125]

Spiritual science, as Rudolf Steiner imparts it, facilitates a new form of supersensible knowledge, with which we can gain an insightful relationship into religious life. Here this is illustrated in just one example, which has a particular connection with the theme of 'growing old'. On 29 April 1923, Rudolf Steiner spoke in Prague about anthroposophy as a path to deeper understanding of the Easter mystery. Starting from the studies of the earth's history by Viennese geologist Eduard Suess, he makes a comparison between scientific and spiritual-scientific enquiry, showing that religion, in particular Christianity, points us to real spiritual renewal.

The Viennese geologist Eduard Suess, an excellent researcher, speaks in his book, *The Face of the Earth*, about how the earth's aspect must once have been completely different from today, when we are really living on a dead earth. The clods of matter on which we walk belong to a dying world. This geologist assumes that the earth was once more alive and has gradually passed over into a dead condition. So here Suess is saying something similar, in a quite different field, to what Christ said in respect of the earth's spiritual life. If all that existed was a future in which the earth was pulverized—if the earth did not resemble the human being, whose body turns to dust yet whose spirit lives on—then we would all go under with its demise. But as we look upon this earth of ours, we are seeing something that will lead us on into Jupiter existence. We see already a new earth.

In terms of physical reality, this view of the earth's demise is correct, but in terms of spirit and soul something else is true. To the old initiates at the time of the mystery of Golgotha it was clear that ancient civilization, the ancient mysteries, had come to an end. The way in which ancient peoples had lived with their gods, and with natural phenomena, was over. But the gods, they saw, send the human being an ability to live toward the future with the spirit. The knowledge and understanding that could be drawn forth from the earth in olden times, had passed. A new age must come when, by their own will and strength, human beings initiate a realm in which dead thinking can be re-enlivened. This was the prophecy at the time of the mystery of Golgotha. This realm can also be outwardly understood and assimilated, albeit only by modern people. We now need to feel that the divine realm, the kingdom of which the Christ speaks, must be seen by us on the earth, where Christ now works. This must be fulfilled on earth, and the fulfilment of the divine kingdom must be accorded serious attention and understanding specifically in our day and age. In all fields we can experience how human beings are beginning to be at risk of becoming sundered from worlds of spirit and from their intrinsic nature if they do not find access to the spiritual world. With conventional science, human beings cannot come near to an understanding of their own human nature. [...]

We achieved I consciousness through unliving thinking, for this could not have been attained with the ancient, living form of thinking. Now we possess this I consciousness, but it has to be inwardly tempered, illumined and spiritualized by saying these words in the right way: 'Not I, but Christ in me.' We must be able to assimilate Christ into this, our inmost being, which we have to acquire through spiritual understanding. As human beings we can only accomplish this if we can imbue ourselves with the true will of anthroposophic life. But anthropsophy, basically, will not seek to be a new religion. Christianity already exists, after all. We are led to Christ, but we do not need to found a new religion for this purpose; we need only a new way in to Christianity. Anthroposophy opens this way for us: it opens up the new and so sorely needed path to understanding the mystery of Golgotha.[126]

> A key moment for this new understanding of Christ is the appearance of this divine being amongst humankind. In the lecture of 15 April 1922, Rudolf Steiner describes the birth and death of Christ as 'a matter of the gods'. Gods sent Christ to the earth 'so that a god might acquaint himself with human death and, with his divine power, vanquish it'. Each person's individual process of maturation and transformation finds its archetype with this participation in cosmic occurrences.

And in the realm of the gods it was resolved to send a god down to earth so that he might pass through death as deity, and inform divine wisdom with this death experience. This is revealed in intuitive vision of the mystery of Golgotha, through which something was accomplished not only for human beings but for gods also. We can say that the gods, who before could speak to earthly human beings only of the mystery of birth, saw how the earth was gradually growing away from those forces they themselves had implanted; they saw how death would grasp hold of the human soul. And therefore they sent Christ to the earth so that a god might acquaint himself with human death and, with his divine power, vanquish it. This is the divine event: the gods, for the sake of their own destiny, on their own behalf, introduced the mystery of Golgotha into the evolution of the cosmos and allowed it to transpire. Previously, everything occurred [for them] in divine, spiritual worlds but now a god descended. And upon the earth was accomplished a super-earthly event within an earthly form. What happened at Golgotha was thus a spiritual event transposed to the earth. That is the important thing we can learn about Christianity through modern, anthroposophic spiritual science.[127]

Modern Gerontology, a Survey

In conclusion, let us come forward into our own day and examine the key questions and concerns around ageing as they are formulated in the modern world, primarily in German-speaking Europe.* In this context we can also consider the degree to which Rudolf Steiner's outlook is still topical and what it might contribute to the debate.

To offer insight into the state of research in this field, below we present some current gerontological studies, and also detail the latest social trends relating to the care of the elderly and very old. These projects and forms of organization are intended to show possible approaches, and where new ideas are either needed or have been implemented. This is a subjective selection, and has nothing to do with how such studies may have been received or adopted in the public and policy domain. Nevertheless, the social relevance of these impulses was the prime criterion for their inclusion. Above all, studies are cited here whose approach is distinguished by an ethical stance of esteem toward people as creative individuals. This sounds self-evident, but is not. Powerful

---

*Although this volume was first published in German and the editor is clearly writing primarily from the perspective of the German-speaking world, we felt that this concluding survey contains sufficient useful material of a general nature to warrant inclusion in the English edition. Given the rapidly-changing situation in the English-speaking world regarding the living conditions and care of ageing and elderly people, the best source of information for the Caring Communities, Culture of Dying and other organizations and associations referred to below is to be found online.

rational mindsets that today hold sway throughout all circumstances and ages suppress the notion of ageing as a 'peripheral' phenomenon. Increasingly, it is thought necessary to prioritize economic viability and efficiency. Only externally measurable benefits and profit factors are thought to count. The human argument is downgraded as something of 'subsidiary importance', with health statistics according importance only to measurable parameters. Our view of the living individual who needs our care is distorted by a burgeoning plethora of rules and ordinances. In Britain, for example, the National Health Service and social services are at breaking point in their efforts to provide care to the elderly. There seems to be little or no room for growing old, and for valuing this stage of life.

And yet there are many research institutes, care- and nursing homes, as well as representatives of the elderly themselves, who speak out on behalf of the aged. Growing numbers of civil society groups and movements work to create successful mixed-generation communities. Their commitment is improving actual daily lives but also extends to pilot studies and the research field. What counts here always are the real lives that people are living.

In general we find that increasing attention is being paid to ageing due to the demographic changes occurring in our society. In economic terms, pensioners are a highly valued consumer group. But beyond this they contribute to greater reflectiveness and deceleration in the hectic pace of modern life, and this is a boon to society. At the same time, these seniors themselves are becoming more aware of their role, seemingly giving expression to what Rudolf Steiner described as the 'awakening of the I'. This is part of the very pulse of our era. Modern people wish to be autonomous and responsible for themselves. Outmoded forms are being questioned, not only by young people, but as an expression of the general *zeitgeist*. Autonomy at the end of life is a widespread desire. But the enormous increase in life expectancy through advancing medical knowledge and surgical techniques can militate against the maturation of a more spiritual outlook in old age. Wherein lies the meaning of such advanced old age? What supports maturation? Gerontology has increasingly allied itself with resilience research. What role is played by our ability to face resistance and endure difficulties? How can we handle the loss of our bodily stability yet remain inwardly content? It will be hard for us to find meaning and fulfilment in old age if we surrender ourselves to suffering and see our condition only in terms of pain and loss. It is therefore easy to tire of life and to see euthanasia as tempting. The Heidelberg study on old age, described in more detail below, highlights the bases for finding value and meaning even in old age and suffering. Where ageing is seen as an important part of a whole life, and where human encounters remain possible into very advanced old age, this can be valuable enrichment for all generations. Rudolf Steiner never tired of pointing to the importance of human encounters and empathy for healthy and fulfilled ageing. In the same way, meditations for developing mindfulness—a current trend referred to earlier—can strengthen psychological health.

The early years of life, with the education and upbringing involved in them, are associated with high costs, and the same is true of old age. It would be the sign of a mature civilization for these costs to be substantially borne by society. But, despite general prosperity, economic pressures are continually growing. Who is to bear the costs?

Care institutions are increasingly at a loss to know how to meet the challenges they face either organizationally or humanly. Amidst this distress, civil society initiatives are emerging to counter diffident and purely cost-oriented perspectives on the elderly. Such 'Caring Communities', working on their own free initiative in an intergenerational way, are meeting with increasing regard and respect. Similarly, efforts are underway to create dementia-friendly living communities. Just as maturational processes only arise through the active involvement of the individuals concerned, so social processes need the involvement of the whole community. The more that human beings themselves take responsibility for these processes, the more sustained will be their effect.

Reports on the situation for the older generation in Germany

In the Federal Republic of Germany, a report on the elderly has been commissioned and published every four years since 1993. The reports are based on high-quality studies of the elderly and very old carried out at universities and research institutes. The questions and issues highlighted in each report are reviewed by an independent commission of experts and serve as ongoing support for decisions and policies relating to the elderly. They are an important source of information about the lives and circumstances of older people, and help stimulate public debate.

Generali studies on the elderly and very old

Discussion about an ageing population depends on clear facts. In the past decade, the Generali studies on old age provided comprehensive empirical data, initially with a study of ageing concerning the living conditions and perspectives of those aged between 65 and 85 in Germany. A survey of over four thousand people was then complemented by a study on the very elderly. Using targeted interviews with people in the '4th age' population group, aged between 85 and 99, the investigators examined specific possibilities and limitations of autonomy and social involvement in advanced old age.

The study findings were incorporated into the federal government's seventh report on ageing, which was published in October 2015, and addressed 'Care and Co-Responsibility in the Community—Ensuring Community Development for the Future'. It sought to offer foundations for 'meeting the needs of the elderly in diverse situations, and supporting as independent a life as possible for them'. At a publication launch of the study on the life of the very elderly, the chair of the experts' commission, the psychologist Andreas Kruse from the Gerontology Institute at Heidelberg University, gave a telling outline of the primary issues and circumstances affecting very old people:

> For the very elderly it feels of existential importance to be an active part of society. They find fulfilment in deep encounters with other people, and this can help them overcome both their inner and outward vulnerability. They have a great desire for more trust, esteem and participation. There are insufficient opportunities for those over 85 to participate in the community.[128]

A chief concern of the study is to correct the general view of old age as a deficiency.

I had the opportunity to listen to talks by Professor Kruse, a gerontologist renowned far beyond Germany, during symposia at the University of Zurich and at events organized by the interdisciplinary 'Palliative Care and Organizational Ethics' association, where he is a regular guest lecturer. His words give pause for thought. Below I quote some of his core views, which I took down during his talks.

—As long as we feel ageing only to be a process of decline, we render it more difficult.
—The way in which the elderly are perceived and described has a discriminatory and humiliating quality.
—The elderly enjoy living in caring relationships. They want to participate in the world, feel themselves to be part of it, and be concerned and involved with something or someone. When this ceases to be possible they are excluded from the world.
—Social relationships are an elixir of life. Intergenerational dialogue is very important.
—Increasing vulnerability in old age can cause high levels of distress.
—Frailty and age are not illness. An illness consciously acknowledged can be an important factor for quality of life in old age.
—Old people should not be 'kept occupied' with something. That takes away their dignity. What is important is to relate to them, be in relationship with them.

In Switzerland, too, there are many gerontology research projects and studies. Below, in necessary brevity, we outline a few of these by way of illustration:

Switzerland Generations Report, 2008:
Generations—Structures and Relationships

Published in 2008 as part of the NFP 52 National Research Programme, the Switzerland Generations Report undertook a broad-based investigation of intergenerational social conditions. The report refutes stereotypical pictures of 'the elderly', and of conflicts between old and young, showing that an increasingly ageing population is changing how generations relate to one another. Co-author of the study was the current Professor Emeritus for Sociology at Zurich University, François Höpflinger, who has made detailed study of intergenerational relationships and their changing demographic. Since 2014 he has been a member of the directorate of the Centre for Gerontology ZfG at Zurich University. His website[129] provides a wealth of information on generational issues.

National 'End of Life' Research Project (NFP 67), 2012–2017

The Swiss Nationalfonds 'End of Life' research project ran for five years. Representatives from the Forum for a New Culture of Dying also took part in several presentation events. The most diverse aspects of end-of-life care were investigated in 33 different projects. Values, spiritual and ethical questions, legal regulations and many practical, medical and nursing issues were addressed in the studies. Their results reflected not only how complex the end of life is for the dying and their relatives, but also the continually changing ways in which we relate to the dying.

In a 'Summing Up' report, also available online,[130] the research results were published and conclusions were drawn, formulated in the form of eleven 'impulses' or actions for reshaping society. Below we present a few selected motifs and ideas from this.

Key importance is given to human relationships. Opportunities for conversation and dialogue are important. Being able to meet others and express oneself enhances quality of life. Involvement with others, inclusion, strengthens people's resilience and is important both for the elderly and for their relatives. Forms of common decision-making in difficult situations need to be practised. The desire for autonomy at the end of life expresses the fact that we do not want to become victims or just 'patients'. (Impulse 3: Implement medical ethics principles, and Impulse 7: Establish monitoring of decisions and practices at the end of life.)

A study undertaken as part of the NFP 67 gave rise to much concern: it investigated what is called 'terminal sedation', the use in palliative care of tranquillizers to put terminal patients into a continuous deep sleep shortly before death. Even though this does not usually shorten the patient's life, terminal sedation is nevertheless an ethically weighty decision, and is being used with increasing frequency. In Switzerland its use increased nearly fourfold between 2001 and 2013. These are very challenging issues, for palliative care is concerned with meeting a patient's individual needs and circumstances at the end of life, and pressing questions arise particularly in relation to pain and suffering. There is a tendency here for the natural process of dying to be overlaid and to some degree inhibited by a well-meaning cloak. The passage from life to death can then only happen unconsciously, and the widely reported light-filled moments before crossing the threshold may then be veiled. It becomes hard to determine when care of the dying becomes euthanasia. The president of the NFP 67 directorate, Dr. Markus Zimmermann, from the department for Moral Theology and Ethics at the University of Fribourg, urged caution and an alertness to these issues, saying that thorough observation of the measures, effects and aims of palliative care was urgently needed. (Impulse 8: Clarification of fundamental criteria of adult protection law.)

The tenth of the eleven impulses emerged from areas of investigation concerned with 'spirituality at the end of life'. This relates to comprehensive care of the whole person at the end of life, not only body-focused measures. Social, psychological and spiritual aspects influence the quality of life of the dying, and ideas drawn from alternative religion are gaining increasing importance. Anthroposophic institutes—such as Paracelsus Hospital in Richterswil, Switzerland, The Christian Community and the 'Culture of Dying' working group—were also surveyed in this context. The report found that:

> Unlike other institutions, anthroposophic ones offer a broad scope of possibility in the spiritual domain. The role of physician is also perceived differently here: patients find that doctors have more time for them than in other hospitals, and develop a strong personal connection with them. Patients value the openness of anthroposophic physicians for religious and spiritual issues. (Impulse 10: Strengthen comprehensive care at the end of life.)

Yet another study that formed part of the NFP 67, and had some relationship to questions of spirituality, concerned 'Waking Visions and Dream Visions at the End of Life'.

Simon Peng-Keller, Professor for Spiritual Care found that patients often have imaginative experiences. He spoke of hyper-real experiences that should not be interpreted as pathology. 87 percent of cases examined involved hyper-real phenomena of this kind, and we should not conclude, he said, that these are caused by delirium and therefore dismiss them as a disorder. In most cases these experiences are meaningful, comforting and sustaining, as well as being comprehensible to others. Even when troubling or burdensome, it can be observed that they nevertheless remain a resource that helps a patient put things in perspective at the end of their life. 'The arduous nature of my situation,' said one patient, 'enabled me to remain inwardly animated.' (Impulse 9: Encourage and support open discussion about dying and death in clinics and palliative care centres.)

Civil society impulses

'Integrated care of the elderly is more than in-patient and out-patient provision!' This striking sentence is worth reflecting on. It comes from the Caring Communities movement, a civil society movement that seeks to redress the isolation of older people in particular, and the lack of care and attention they receive.

In 1986, the World Health Organization held its first international conference on healthcare, and passed the Ottawa Health Charter, with the aim of implementing the 'Health for All' strategy by the year 2000. This was the first impetus for the Caring Communities movement that is now growing in many countries. In 2018, many smaller and larger platforms have now arisen to promote Caring Communities. For instance, the Migros Cooperative Association has issued this statement about its projects to create better meeting places within local communities:

> Urbanization, globalization, digitalization, social acceleration and increasing social mobility summon a need in society for things that are familiar, local and within the scope of action of individuals themselves, so as to sustain quality of life at the micro level. Neighbourliness and Caring Communities are becoming ever more important in the face of these demographic changes.[131]

And in June 2018, over 140 participants from Switzerland and neighbouring countries held a network meeting of the Cooperative Association in Zurich, to discuss the ideas, aims and values of Caring Communities. Many of the activists who attended were united in their concern at the increasing management structures and bureaucratization of the movement. The important thing, they said, was to create relationships of trust in neighbourhoods. The 'Neighbourhood Solidarity' project, for instance, already has two years' experience in such developments. Active in particular in western Switzerland, it promotes community solidarity and neighbourhood support.

Similar events are held also in Germany and Austria. For instance, in Germany in 2013 a conference of experts in the field considered 'Caring Communities—From Founding Idea to Action Projects'. And in Austria, the Caring Communities movement, with the Institute for Palliative Care and Organizational Ethics, has a centre at Vienna's IFF (Faculty for Interdisciplinary Research and Further Training). Caring Communities are on the increase, and these are important developments.

★★★

Perusing this survey of contemporary gerontology, and the efforts underway today to understand maturation processes and the support and development of resilience, it is clear that Rudolf Steiner's focus on ageing has lost nothing of its topicality. In fact, many symptoms which he described in his day have since become exacerbated. Given the increasing rates of dementia, Steiner's ideas about measures that can be taken in youth already for preventing age-related conditions, are likewise very relevant. His concern for intergenerational social impulses is gaining new momentum through the Caring Communities movement. But with the changing demographic, and the increase in the scope of medical interventions, the most pressing concern for the old relates to end-of-life care. The ethical and individual questions raised by wider availability of intervention are challenging. What is a 'natural' death? What do I think about extending or shortening life? What is happening to our past ethical norms and what guidelines can we find here? It is apparent from efforts to enhance mindfulness in all phases of life that there is a yearning to find answers also for the existential and spiritual issues that relate to these questions. I hope that dialogue on these themes can become ever more fruitful.

Notes

For consistency of language and style, German texts from Rudolf Steiner have been translated afresh. Thus, page references refer to the German editions. However, published English translations, listed by the Collected Works ('GA' number), are given on p. 231f.

1. See for instance GA 110.
2. In an interview with Peter Böhnel, 'Open for New Impressions in Old Age' in *Forum. Das Wochenmagazin*, 23 February 2018, available online at: https://magazin-forum.de/de/de/node/8015. For more on Kruse himself see the chapter 'Modern Gerontology, a Survey', p. 213.
3. From a lecture in Berlin on 5 December 1912, GA 62, p. 184, here quoted as in GA 40, p. 215.
4. *Die Geheimwissenschaft im Umriss (Occult Science)*, GA 13, p. 191.
5. Lecture in Stuttgart, 15 June 1919, GA 192, p. 194.
6. Lecture in Dornach, 11 December 1920, GA 202, pp. 110–114.
7. Lecture in Munich, 25 August 1911, GA 129, p. 173f.
8. Lecture in Dornach, 12 October 1919, GA 191, p. 115.
9. Lecture in Hannover, 18 November 1912, GA 140, pp. 41–43.
10. Lecture in Munich, 15 February 1918, GA 271, p. 87.
11. Lecture in Berlin, 21 May 1918, GA 181, p. 266f.
12. In a lecture in Berlin, 7 December 1915, GA 157a, p. 94.
13. Lecture in Berlin, 21 May 1918, GA 181, p. 267.
14. Lecture in Dornach, 11 January 1918, GA 180.
15. Lecture in Berlin, 7 December 1915, GA 157a, p. 93f.
16. Lecture in Dornach, 11 January 1918, GA 180, p. 209f.
17. Lecture in Berlin, 21 May 1918, GA 181, p. 265.

18. Lecture in Dornach, 6 January 1918, GA 180, p. 187f.

19. This lecture was published in revised form in the April issue of the journal *Lucifer-Gnosis* (GA 34, pp. 309–348).

20. Lecture in Berlin, 28 February 1907, GA 55, pp. 170–173.

21. Lecture in Zurich, 4 February 1919, GA 193, pp. 22–25.

22. Lecture in Dornach, 22 April 1923, GA 306, pp. 164–166.

23. Lecture in Stuttgart, 26 March 1923, GA 304a, p. 51f.

24. Lecture in Kassel, 29 January 1912, GA 130, p. 242f.

25. Lecture in Dornach, 11 March 1923, GA 222, p. 17f.

26. Lecture in Dornach, 12 March 1923, GA 222, p. 40f.

27. Lecture in Berlin, 28 October 1909, GA 58, pp. 137–141.

28. Lecture in Berlin, 22 December 1909, GA 116, p. 45f.

29. Lecture in Stuttgart, 28 September 1919, GA 192, p. 386.

30. Lecture in Stuttgart, 26 March 1923, GA 304a, p. 47.

31. Answers to questions, The Hague, 12 April 1922, GA 342a, p. 215f.

32. Lecture in Berlin, 23 April 1914, GA 63, p. 410.

33. Lecture in Zurich, 9 October 1918, GA 182, p. 138f.

34. Lecture in Dornach, 15 December 1917, GA 179, pp. 101–103.

35. Lecture in Zurich, 6 November 1917, GA 178, pp. 78–80.

36. Lecture in Leipzig, 22 February 1916, GA 168. pp. 80–82.

37. Lecture in Berlin, 23 April 1914, GA 63, pp. 409–411.

38. Lecture in Berlin, 2 November 1908, GA 107, pp. 93–102.

39. Lecture in Heidenheim, 29 April 1918, GA 182, p. 74f.

40. Lecture in Zurich, 31 January 1915, GA 159, p. 23f.

41. Lecture in Dornach, 18 March 1923, GA 222, p. 89.

42. Lecture in Stuttgart, 4 October 1922, GA 217, p. 31.

43. Lecture in Munich, 2 May 1918, GA 174a, p. 250f.

44. Lecture in Stuttgart, 26 April 1918, GA 174b, pp. 335–341.

45. Lecture in Dornach, 26 December 1921, GA 303, p. 62–64.

46. Ibid, pp. 64–67.

47. See the related sketch below from a board drawing by Rudolf Steiner.

48. Lecture in Dornach, 12 January 1918, GA 180, pp. 237–245.
49. Lecture in Pforzheim, 30 January 1910, GA 118, p. 55.
50. Lecture in Stuttgart, 28 August 1919, GA 293, pp. 106–108.
51. Ibid, p. 111f.
52. Lecture in Dornach, 14 September 1918, GA 184, pp. 106–110.
53. Lecture in Torquay, 16 August 1924, GA 243, pp. 132–134.
54. Lecture in Berlin, 2 April 1918, GA 181, p. 184f.
55. Lecture in Dornach, 28 June 1923, GA 350, pp. 154–157.
56. Lecture in Dornach, 8 October 1920, GA 314, pp. 39–42.
57. Lecture in Dornach, 24 October 1922, GA 348, p. 54f.
58. Lecture in London, 29 August 1924, GA 319, p. 238f.
59. Lecture in The Hague, 16 November 1923, GA 319, p. 116f.
60. Lecture in Dornach, 16 January 1920, GA 196, p. 69f.
61. Lecture in Dornach, 15 July 1921, GA 205, p.192f.
62. Lecture in Dornach, 2 April 1920, GA 312, p. 257f.
63. Lecture in Dornach, 20 February 1924, GA 352, pp. 141–143.
64. Ibid, pp. 144–145.
65. Ibid, pp. 145–147.
66. Lecture in Berlin, 31 January 1907, GA 55, p. 144f.
67. Lecture in Vienna, 21 January 1913, GA 140, p. 154.
68. Lecture in Berlin, 11 February 1913, GA 141, p. 140.
69. Lecture in Dornach, 12 April 1921, GA 313, pp. 39–41.
70. Ibid, p. 42.
71. Lecture in Berlin, 13 December 1906, GA 55, pp. 109–111.

72. Lecture in Kassel, 6 July 1909, GA 112, p. 253.

73. Lecture in Berlin, 16 November 1915, GA 157a, p. 21.

74. Lecture in Dornach, 5 September 1915, GA 163, pp. 111–121.

75. Lecture in Stuttgart, 20 February 1913, GA 140, pp. 2167–219.

76. Lecture in Munich, 10 March 1913, GA 140, pp. 259–261.

77. Lecture in Nuremberg, 10 February 1918, GA 182, pp. 52–54.

78. Lecture in Stockholm, 8 June 1913, GA 150, p. 73f.

79. Lecture in Leipzig, 4 July 1906, GA 94, p. 155f.

80. Lecture in Vienna, 8 February 1912, GA 130, p. 254f.

81. Lecture in Dornach, 1 March 1924, GA 235, p. 96f.

82. Lecture in Bern, 22 December 1909, GA 116, p. 42.

83. Lecture in Berlin, 22 December 1909, GA 116, p. 42.

84. Lecture in Berlin, 18 November 1915, GA 157a, pp. 49–51.

85. Lecture in Dornach, 1 January 1922, GA 210, p. 20f.

86. Lecture in Dornach, 29 January 1921, GA 203, pp. 135–137.

87. Lecture in Augsburg, 14 March 1913, GA 150, p. 25f.

88. Lecture in Munich, 30 August 1913, GA 147, pp. 118–120.

89. Lecture in Dornach, 5 October 1919, GA 191, pp. 61–63.

90. Lecture in Stuttgart, 23 August 1919, GA 293, p. 53f.

91. Lecture in Munich, 14 February 1918, GA 174a, pp. 213–216.

92. Lecture in Bergen, 10 October 1913, GA 140, p. 329f.

93. The first verse of a poem that Goethe wrote in Lauterbrunnen in 1779, nowadays known by the title 'Song of the Spirits Over the Waters' (*Goethes Werke*, vol. 1: *Gedichte und Epen 1*, ed. by Erich Trunz, Munich 1981, p. 143).

94. Lecture in Dornach, 26 June 1921, GA 205, p. 79f.

95. Lecture in Budapest, 6 June 1909, GA 109/111, p. 196.

96. Lecture in Heidenheim, 12 June 1919, GA 193, pp. 92–94.

97. Lecture in Berlin, 16 November 1915, GA 157a, p. 29f.

98. Lecture in Berlin, 2 April 1918, GA 181, p. 193f.

99. Lecture in Kristiania (Oslo), 17 May 1923 (morning), GA 226, p. 36f.
100. Lecture in London, 19 November 1922, GA 218, p. 169.
101. Lecture in Berlin, 19 December 1915, GA 165, p. 20f.
102. In a lecture in London, 2 September 1923, GA 228, p. 82.
103. Lecture in Dornach, 21 January 1921, GA 203, p. 83.
104. Ibid, p. 86.
105. Lecture in Zurich, 10 October 1916, GA 168, pp. 96–98.
106. Ibid, p. 107.
107. Lecture in Vienna, 29 September 1923, GA 84, pp. 258, 260.
108. Lecture in Berlin, 29 January 1918, GA 181, pp. 38–40.
109. Lecture in Stuttgart, 12 October 1922, GA 217, pp. 152–155.
110. Lecture in Dornach, 22 January 1921, GA 203, pp. 99–101.
111. Lecture in Wiesbaden, 7 January 1911, GA 127, p. 40f.
112. Lecture in Dornach, 26 December 1921, GA 303, p. 61f.
113. Lecture in The Hague, 14 November 1923, GA 304a, p. 117.
114. Lecture in Dornach, 21 October 1917, GA 177, p. 197f.
115. Lecture in Stuttgart, 11 April 1924, GA 308, pp. 87–89.
116. For Marie Steiner, 25 December 1922, GA 40, p. 107.
117. Lecture in Dornach, 31 December 1922, GA 219, p. 190f.
118. Lecture in Kristiania (Oslo), 16 May 1923, GA 226, p. 21f.
119. Lecture in Dornach, 2 January 1915, GA 275, p. 127.
120. Lecture in Bern, 4 November 1919, GA 193, pp. 209–211.
121. Lecture In Dornach, 12 October 1919, GA 191, p. 121f.
122. Lecture in Dornach, 23 March 1923, GA 222, pp. 119, 121.
123. Lecture in Dornach, 26 October 1917, GA 177, p. 221.
124. Lecture in Dornach, 15 November, 1919, GA 191, p. 280.
125. Lecture in Dornach, 17 October 1919, GA 191, p. 134.
126. Lecture in Prague, 29 April 1923, GA 224, pp. 140–142.
127. Lecture in London, 15 April 1922, GA 211, p. 179f.
128. Press release from the Generali Zukunftsfonds on its study of the very elderly, 20 March 2014. Available online at: https://www.generali.de/ueber-generali/presse-medien/

pressemitteilungen/generali-hochaltrigenstudie—aktiver-teil-der-gesellschaft-zu-sein-ist-fuer-hochaltirige-existentiell–10108

129. www/hoepflinger.com

130. 'Lebensende. Synthesebericht des Nationalen Forschungsprogramms NFP 67', ed. by the NFP 67 directorate, Schweizerischer Nationalfonds, Bern 2017. Available online at: http://www.nfp67.ch/SiteCollectionDocuments/nfp67-synthesebericht-de.pdf. A survey of the NFP 67 'Impulses' is reprinted there in section 3, p. 50–53.

131. Migros-Genossenschaft-Bund, Direktion Kultur und Soziales, über das Thema 'Begegnungsort'. Available online at: www.migros-kulturprozent.ch/uber-uns/organisation/direktion-kultur-und-soziales/gesellschaft/unsere-themen/begegnungsort

Sources

The following volumes are cited in this book. Where relevant, published editions of equivalent English translations are provided.

The works of Rudolf Steiner are listed with the volume numbers of the complete works in German, the *Gesamtausgabe* (GA), as published by Rudolf Steiner Verlag, Dornach, Switzerland.

RSP = Rudolf Steiner Press, UK
AP / SB = Anthroposophic Press / SteinerBooks, USA

GA

13	*Occult Science* (RSP) / *An Outline of Esoteric Science* (SB)
34	*Lucifer-Gnosis; Grundlegende Aufsätze zur Anthroposophie und Berichte aus den Zeitschriften 'Luzifer' und 'Lucifer–Gnosis' 1903–1908*
40	*Wahrspruchworte*
55	*Supersensible Knowledge* (AP / RSP)
58	*Transforming the Soul, Vol. 1* (RSP)
62	*Ergebnisse der Geistesforschung*
63	*Geisteswissenschaft als Lebensgut*
84	*Was wollte das Goetheanum und was soll die Anthroposophie?*
94	*An Esoteric Cosmolgy* (SB)
107	*Disease, Karma and Healing* (RSP)
109/111	*Rosicrucian Esotericism* (AP)/*Principle of Spiritual Economy* (AP)
110	*Spiritual Hierarchies and Their Reflection in the Spiritual World* (AP)
112	*Gospel of St John in relation to the other Gospels* (AP)
116	*The Christ Impulse* (RSP)
118	*Das Ereignis der Christus-Erscheinung in der ätherischen Welt*
127	*Die Mission der neuen Geistesoffenbarung*
129	*Wonders of the World* (RSP)

205   *Therapeutic Insights: Earthly and Cosmic Laws* (Mercury Press)
210   *Old and New Methods of Initiation* (RSP)
211   *Sun Mystery and the Mystery of Death and Resurrection* (SB)
217   *Becoming the Archangel Michael's Companions* (SB)
218   *Spirit as Sculptor of the Human Organism* (RSP)
219   *Man and the World of Stars* (AP)
222   *The Driving Force of Spiritual Powers* (SB)
224   *Die menschliche Seele in ihrem Zusammenhang mit göttlich-geistigen Individualitäten. Die Verinnerlichung der Jahresfeste*
226   *Man's Being, His Destiny and World Evolution* (AP)
228   *Initiation Science* (RSP)
235   *Karmic Relationships, Vol. 1* (RSP)
243   *True and False Paths in Spiritual Investigation* (RSP)
271   *Kunst und Kunsterkenntnis. Grundlagen einer neuen Ästhetik*
275   *Art as Seen in the Light of Mystery Wisdom* (RSP)
293   *Study of Man* (RSP)/*The Foundations of Human Experience* (SB)
303   *Soul Economy and Waldorf Education* (AP/RSP)
304a *Waldorf Education and Anthroposophy, Vol. 2* (AP)
306   *The Child's Changing Consciousness* (AP)
308   *The Essentials of Education* (AP)
312   *Introducing Anthroposophical Medicine* (SB)
313   *Illness and Therapy* (RSP)
314   *Physiology and Healing* (RSP)
319   *The Healing Process* (SB)
324a *The Fourth Dimension* (SB)
348   *From Comets to Cocaine* (RSP)
350   *From Mammoths to Mediums* (RSP)
352   *From Elephants to Einstein* (RSP)

All English-language titles are available via Rudolf Steiner Press, UK (www.rudolfsteinerpress.com) or SteinerBooks, USA (www.steinerbooks.org)

A NOTE FROM RUDOLF STEINER PRESS

We are an independent publisher and registered charity (non-profit organisation) dedicated to making available the work of Rudolf Steiner in English translation. We care a great deal about the content of our books and have hundreds of titles available – as printed books, ebooks and in audio formats.

As a publisher devoted to anthroposophy...

- We continually commission translations of previously unpublished works by Rudolf Steiner and invest in re-translating, editing and improving our editions.

- We are committed to making anthroposophy available to all by publishing introductory books as well as contemporary research.

- Our new print editions and ebooks are carefully checked and proofread for accuracy, and converted into all formats for all platforms.

- Our translations are officially authorised by Rudolf Steiner's estate in Dornach, Switzerland, to whom we pay royalties on sales, thus assisting their critical work.

So, look out for Rudolf Steiner Press as a mark of quality and support us today by buying our books, or contact us should you wish to sponsor specific titles or to support the charity with a gift or legacy.

office@rudolfsteinerpress.com
Join our e-mailing list at www.rudolfsteinerpress.com

RUDOLF STEINER PRESS